TO KONY,

♡-FULLY,

WITH LOVE!

Roger

MW00917768

NexGen Human

A Modern Age Path to Fulfillment

ROGER KENNETH MARSH

authorHOUSE®

AuthorHouse™
1663 Liberty Drive, Suite 200
Bloomington, IN 47403
www.authorhouse.com
Phone: 1-800-839-8640

© 2008 Roger Kenneth Marsh. All rights reserved.

No part of this book may be reproduced, stored in a retrieval system, or transmitted by any means without the written permission of the author.

First published by AuthorHouse 10/21/2008

ISBN: 978-1-4389-0372-9 (sc)

Library of Congress Control Number: 2008908564

Printed in the United States of America
Bloomington, Indiana

This book is printed on acid-free paper.

Prayer for a NexGen Human

I embrace the adventure that is my life
I rejoice in its challenges
I rejoice in its opportunities
Through all my ups and through all my downs
I am strengthened on my journey
As I deepen my Connections
I unfold and discover
Who I am
And deliver my gifts
To the world
I embrace the adventure that is my life!

This book is dedicated to God, Universal Intelligence, Great Spirit, Source. Thank you for inspiring me to follow your invisible footsteps. Thank you for surrounding me with love. Thank you for giving me the eyes to see it.

This book is also dedicated to my many teachers, mentors, role models, friends, and loved ones. Thank you for believing in me. Thank you for supporting me. Thank you for shining your light and helping me see the way.

And finally, this book is dedicated to NexGen Humans all over the world. Thank you for having the compassion and courage to follow your deepest desires. Thank you for waking up and being true to something larger than yourself. Thank you for making a difference.

Contents

Introduction

ful◆fill◆ment : 1. to carry out (a promise, etc.) 2. to do (a duty, etc.) 3. to satisfy (a condition) 4. to bring to an end; complete.

The path of a NexGen Human is a modern age path to *fulfillment.* Which is really what we all want, isn't it? Of all the things we pursue and all the things we do, ultimately what we're seeking and striving for is fulfillment. However, somehow it seems that today, the seeking and striving has gotten more and more difficult, and the experience of fulfillment more and more rare.

Look at the definition for fulfillment one more time. Isn't it interesting that in the thing we're all seeking, are things like carrying out a promise, doing a duty, satisfying a condition, bringing to an end, and completing. That doesn't sound all that great, does it? In fact, that kind of sounds like hard work. But I'd like you to consider that from a different perspective, this definition of fulfillment is exactly accurate, and is exactly what we are looking for. As it is defined right here, it *is* the access to the fulfillment in life we all so desire. How can that be?

You are here for a reason. You have a purpose. Once you are on that path and *fulfilling* your destiny – carrying out your promise, doing your duty, satisfying your conditions, completing what you are here to complete - you will experience the fulfillment you desire. The problem is, many of us are carrying out someone else's promise, doing someone else's duty, satisfying someone else's conditions, and not at all completing what we are here to complete. And therein lies the root of our suffering.

The path out of this dilemma is the path of the NexGen Human. It is the Modern Age Hero's Journey. Make no mistake, this is not a journey for the weak at heart. Those weak at heart will not make it. The barriers and challenges are many, but in NO WAY are they insurmountable. This is also not a "quick fix" instant answer to all your problems. It is, however, a long term answer. Which is ultimately the answer you want.

Through this book I will guide you on a journey and exploration called NexGen Human. I will show you a map of the Modern Age Hero's Journey. The terrain you travel will be your own, but the map remains the same – providing direction and guidance, pointing out pitfalls, distinguishing milestones, showing you the peaks and valleys, and the treasures along the way. I have been traveling this path of my own for many years, and while it's an ongoing evolution, I have found what I was looking for. It is my greatest joy that you do too.

The fact that you've been attracted to *this* book, with its very unique cover and unusual title really says something about you, your interests, and what's next for you. Whether you've been on your path of personal transformation and evolution for a long time, or if you're just now consciously stepping onto the path, this book has something to offer you.

If you are ready to develop the critical skills to thrive in the 21st Century … if you are ready to consciously participate in your evolution and embrace your destiny … if you are ready to embark on the journey of a lifetime … then I welcome you, I honor you, and I embrace you as a *NexGen Human*.

Chapter I

THE CRITICAL SKILL

The need for a new skill is emerging.
This critical new skill is a core competency of the NexGen Human.

As a global society we are well into a major transition as the industrial age gives way to the information age. This transition involves a major change in both our strengths and our values as the emphasis shifts from the tangible to the intangible. Our sense of value in the information age is based more on what we know rather than on what we have. We are moving out of an industrial-physical-tangible focus and into an information-nonphysical-intangible focus. As we make this transition, the need for a new skill is emerging.

Historically, certain advanced and trailblazing human beings have accessed and developed this crucial skill. So, in one sense, this is not a new development, however, for the grand majority of us, it is absolutely new. The early pioneers came from all parts of the world and from many different disciplines. They were some of the most influential and satisfied human beings to ever live. We are able to study them, celebrate their successes, and stand on their shoulders. We are part of the evolution - what was once impossible or undreamed of becomes possible, real, and ever more available to those of us who follow the path blazed by these pioneers. Climbing Mt. Everest was once out of the question just as visiting the moon was humanly impossible. Even ice cream, automobiles, and electricity were once luxuries available to only a privileged few, and yet they are now widely available to all. In the same manner, this critical new skill is becoming available to more and more people, including you, if you choose it. Evolutionary energy and intelligence itself is on the move—in, around, and through you and me.

So what is this critical skill? It is the ability to *consciously and consistently partner with the power of the Universe.* It's time for us, both collectively and individually, to develop the skill of joining forces with the Ultimate, most valuable, intangible element in our Universe – the intelligent energy of the Universe itself.

This is a skill you can learn, and develop, to bring the power of this amazing Universal Intelligence alive in your life.

Fundamentally what this means is to shift our idea and *experience* of God, Universal Intelligence, Great Spirit, Source, from an external concept, to an internal reality. No longer is God something outside of us whose existence we must take on the word of others and have faith and *believe* in. Like having someone fall in love for you and then telling you how it is, the old way of relating to God was one step removed. When you don't have the direct experience of God the relationship must be based on faith and belief. Universal Life Force is already in you and is *always* available, but it's up to you to heed the call and maximize your partnership with this force, this intelligence, this energy.

Using new words to describe this energy,
this experience, this "entity," is part of our evolution.

Note that I am deliberately using multiple words to point to this thing we have historically called "God." God, as a word, is a good word, however it has picked up a lot of baggage over the years, has many meanings and forms, and you never know how someone will interpret it. Using new words to describe this energy, this experience, this "entity," is part of our evolution. NexGen Humans evolve beyond these limitations by connecting personally and directly with Source. In this manner they become free of preconceived notions and open up to the actual *experience*, beyond all words, thoughts, and concepts.

WHAT'S YOUR LIFE WORTH LIVING FOR?

There are capacities arising in you that want to express
through you in this time. That want to come alive through you
in this moment on the planet. This is the essence of evolution itself.
The Evolutionary Impulse.

Did you know that approximately 60 billion people have already come and gone on this planet prior to your arrival, leading to you, here now, in this moment? That's 60 thousand million people!

Why you and why now?

What's been going on over all these thousands of years that humans have been present on this earth? What is unique about THIS time in our human evolution? And what does our full participation and engagement look like?

Consider this: specific, innate capacities have begun to arise in the human species that want to express through you in this time. These new capacities want to come alive through you in this moment on the planet. This is the essence of evolution itself. Consider that discovering, embracing, and developing these capacities is the greatest opportunity of your life. You can be an active, conscious partner in this process, for yourself and *others*. This is perhaps the first time in human history that this opportunity is occurring at a conscious level and, therefore, is available to you for the choosing!

Now let's be clear - you don't have to do anything; these new developments do not come with requirements or rules or performance measures you must meet. No one stands in judgment of you and how you live your life except yourself. This is simply a *choice you make*. Why? Because you are uniquely and authentically *impelled and inspired* to do so.

Is it easy? Not always.
Is it worth it? Absolutely.

At some point you will join the 60 billion people who have come and gone before you on this planet. What, before you leave, is your life worth living for?" What is it that is uniquely yours, for you to embrace and express in this time? When you develop this critical skill of partnering with the intelligent energy of the Universe you'll *know* what your life is worth living for. Your life path is uniquely yours, no one can live it for you, and no one knows (except *you* through Universal Intelligence) what your life is all about. Creating a strong partnership with the power of the

Creating a New Context

One of the very valuable things you'll get from reading this book is a new context for living your life.

There's an old saying "context is decisive." I don't know who said this, but whoever did really knew something.

Context is the frame within which we see ourselves and the world. And when we say "context is decisive" what we are saying is that "how we look at the world, who we are, and what we are doing, will determine everything – our results, our experience, our life."

Context *is* decisive.

Let me give you an age-old example that demonstrates the power of this phenomenon: two stone-masons are chipping stones forming blocks for a project they are both working on. A bystander walks up to one stone mason and asks him "What are you doing?" The stone mason looks up wearily from his work and with exasperation states "I am chipping stones." The bystander then approaches the other stone mason and asks the same question "What are you doing? This second stone mason energetically looks up from his work with a smile on his face and says "I am building a castle."

Take a look at your own life. Are you chipping stones? Or are you building a castle? The two stone masons are performing the exact same activity, however they are working inside of two totally different worlds, two totally different CONTEXTS. Can you see what a huge difference this makes?

A powerful context is a different mind-set that literally gives life and purpose to each and every task – it gives meaning. And, very importantly, it provides access to energy and enthusiasm that comes from engaging, and being a part of, an inspiring vision. Without a compelling CONTEXT for your life, it's easy to see how it will simply feel like chipping stones.

The context for a NexGen Human is one of the biggest, one of the most inspiring, and one of the most exciting – engaging the Hero's Journey and your own personal evolutionary path opening up to new and greater depths of love, freedom, trust, inspiration, and fulfillment.

I invite you to take a look at the current context for your life. Is it inspiring, is it energizing, is it compelling?

NexGen Humans are not chipping stones, they are definitely building a castle.

Universe is essential to knowing and living your greatest life. This is now possible and available like never before.

> *In the pages that follow you will discover the NexGen Human*
> *that you are and fully embrace your role in human history,*
> *living your life to its fullest, and expressing and evolving*
> *the cutting edge capacities and gifts uniquely available*
> *to you, in your life, at this time.*

At this point you might be thinking this sounds like a monumental task, one that you may not be up for. It is important to understand that while the IMPACT of this transformation is monumental, the process of actually doing it is as natural as life itself – "it" wants to happen – your task is mostly about getting out of the way and allowing it. The power and energy to get this done is bigger and beyond you – "you" don't have to do it, you just have to get yourself out of the way, that's your task, and that's what this book will help you do.

Can it be hard? Yes. Can it be easy? Yes. Can it be scary? Sure. Can it be exciting and exhilarating? Absolutely! Are there ups and downs? Indeed. It's a journey! And an amazing one at that. So don't worry about how hard it may seem and whether you can do it or not. You can. As many of my teachers have said to me "If you can't believe in you, let me believe in you, and you just trust in that."

As you contemplate developing this new skill and truly living your most powerful and authentic life, consider the following questions:

+ Are you truly happy in your life? Or are you perhaps comfortably bored, or stressed-out?

+ Do you know why you are here living the life you are? Or do you still wonder about that?

+ Are you part of something bigger? Or do you feel relatively separate, making a go of it on your own?

+ Does your energy flow naturally and inspire you to action? Or do you rely more on discipline, forcing and pushing yourself to make it through the day?

+ Do you spontaneously experience love and gratitude? Or is that a relatively rare and conditional experience?

+ Are you able to create and have everything you want and need? Or are you often frustrated and confused in your efforts?

+ Are you satisfied with traditional sources of inspiration and meaning? Or are they no longer working for you, if they ever did?

+ Have you achieved a lot in your life, but yet somehow still experience an emptiness inside, that you know won't be fulfilled with more of the same?

These questions will give you a sense of what's possible through this partnership and help you identify areas of your life you may want to focus on.

Is "life as usual" no longer as satisfying as it once was? Do you sense there is something more? If you are open minded, seeking, and willing to explore new ways of thinking, being, perceiving, and relating, then you are likely ready to develop and deepen your partnership with Universal Life Force.

Only you can answer these questions for yourself.

You are your own authority.

NOW STOP. RIGHT HERE, RIGHT NOW. TAKE A DEEP BREATH AND FOCUS YOUR AWARENESS INSIDE. After reading this far, do you sense something greater opening up and available to you? Do you sense even the smallest amount of possibility or new energy and excitement, somewhere, somehow, twinkling inside you? Close your eyes and just listen inside. What is wanting to evolve through you?

THE 21ST CENTURY HERO'S JOURNEY

At its core, what we are talking about here is the classic Hero's Journey that Joseph Campbell made so famous with his book *The Hero with a Thousand Faces*. However, while its core may remain the same, on its surface even the timeless Hero's Journey is evolving. The Hero's Journey of the Industrial Age, of the 20th Century, was captured in the well known saying "Rags to Riches." Going from material, physical lack, to material, physical abundance. This "Rags to Riches" journey was mostly a journey in the external world with success externally defined and measured. If you completed this journey, it was assumed that happiness would be yours. Whether you actually were or not is a whole other question!

The Hero's Journey of the Information Age, of the 21st Century, is the journey from Isolation-to-Integration.

Or, speaking more tongue-in-cheek, from "Poor Suffering Bastard" to "Divinely Inspired Being" (Note: please don't take this personally – I'm trying to make a point, and I am using strong language for contrast and emphasis. *You* are a Divinely Inspired Being, but we all have areas of our lives, some more than others, where we are "Poor Suffering Bastards."

ON THE PATH OF THE HERO'S JOURNEY

So in this chapter we are talking about the modern age Hero's Journey. One thing I want to point out is that this is a journey that takes a life time. It's not like you go on the journey, arrive at the destination and you're done. You're never done. And that's a good thing. There is always more of you to discover, more to the Universe that you live in, more unfolding of yourself to happen. That's the process, that's the joy, that's the opportunity.

Some of you reading this book may have been on your path of personal growth and evolution for quite some time. Others perhaps are brand new to this thing called self help or personal growth. Either way, I want to be clear it's an ongoing, forever unfolding, path you are on.

Now, life itself <u>will</u> evolve you. You may have noticed you cannot hide from life, try as you might, change happens and you must respond. So everyone in this life grows and changes to some extent, regardless. But you can also accelerate and participate in your own evolution, and not be waiting for life to do it to you. Rather you can proactively seek and create opportunities for your own growth, evolution and expansion. Why would you do this? Because learning and growing is one of the most

satisfying experiences we can have as conscious beings living in this life.

As we go deeper and deeper into ourselves, and expand our awareness and consciousness to wider and wider states, we experience increasing levels of joy and happiness. And as you do this for yourself, you can do this for others. As you grow yourself you are better able to empower others and uplift and expand <u>them</u> to greater and greater levels of joy, love, and happiness.

So the Hero's Journey is really <u>your own</u> personal journey of self discovery, knowledge, growth, and transformation. It's your personal exploration of the mystery of life, of your life, and coming to know more and more, who and what you really are.

It's very important to know that there are lots of pathways to take on this journey. I've done a lot of personal growth and transformational programs, investing far more than $100K in my own transformation, not too mention significant amounts of time and energy. And every little bit of it has been absolutely worth it. But one thing I've learned, and I want you to know, is ultimately they all lead to the same place – back to YOU. So don't worry about taking "the right" pathway. You cannot get lost. It's more important to just get on the path. All of the pathways are essentially facilitating the same thing in different ways – self knowledge – or knowing yourself at deeper and deeper and more powerful levels.

Having experienced many personal growth and transformational programs, one of the common myths and misperceptions I want to dispel for you right here, especially for people brand new to personal growth and development, is the myth, or belief, or fantasy, that you will participate in one program and be transformed. For some reason, when we are new to the path of personal growth, we have this unrealistic fantasy that there is some magic pill or program out there we can take and all our problems will be gone and we'll live happily ever after. But that just isn't how it works.

It's common when someone steps up and outside of the status quo that others around him or her will quiz, question, prod, and joke with the person after the person has done the program "So are you all transformed now?" "Are you a happy person now with all your problems solved?" This reaction is normal, and it's based in fear, fear of change, and fear of their own change and resistance to their own growth and evolution. Because if you challenge yourself, face your fears, and

step up and out of the norm, then they might have to also.

I have coached individuals in relationships where the person I am coaching wants to grow, but their partner is trying to hold them back. This is challenging, but the key is really compassion for the person who is basically afraid of the unknown and is afraid of losing control. So it's really a matter of reassuring them you are only interested in becoming more of who you are, and continue to invite them to discover the same in themselves. This is leadership. Understand that growth and transformation is what we most want as human beings, but it's also what we most fear. This is natural, and to the extent you understand this, you'll be stronger in the face of resistance, both in yourself and in others.

And again, the thing to know is it's a life long process. It's not something you do once and it's over. There is no one program that has all the answers, however they will all provide you something.

For example through one program I became free of my past, through another program I discovered my heart, through another program I found power and confidence in my masculinity, in another program I uncovered deeply held subconscious limiting beliefs, in another program I deepened my spiritual connection, and on, and on, and on. No one program or book has it all. So I encourage you to explore, and play, and customize your own path of personal growth and transformation. And create your very own mosaic of life, your life. There are more opportunities available for this than at any other time in history!

And it is my intention this book, as well as all the programs and products of Beyond Belief, are solid stepping stones on your path. If you are new on this path, I hope this book opens you up to it and really gets you going. And if you are an experienced journeyer, I hope this book provides a new context and perhaps some new milestones to reach for. This is after all, the modern age Hero's Journey, and no matter how far you've come, there is always more to go.

The word bastard here, while it may seem harsh, is perfect since it means one who is "illegitimate, a sham, or inferior." No matter who you are, in any area of your life, that's just not the truth....hence the journey).

The journey from Isolation-to-Integration is a journey with many dimensions and includes the journey from Head-to-Heart, from Thinking-to-Knowing, from Control-to-Trust, from Doing-to-Being, from Physical-to-Metaphysical, from Fear-to-Love, and ultimately integrating them all. And let me be clear that this new journey does not deny the pleasures one can experience by obtaining material things – I am a huge fan of the physical world and the wonderful, magical things we can create, purchase, have, and consume. In fact, a major theme on the life path of a NexGen Human is creation in the physical world. If you think of the well known "Maslow's Hierarchy of Needs," you'll remember there is a baseline of physical world needs that must be met before one can journey any further. In my experience this model is valid; one *does* need a baseline of physical world goods (food, shelter, clothing) from which to venture forward. Consider this your base camp. And while this new journey does require these physical world basics, your success will be measured more internally than externally, more inwardly than outwardly. It's a journey solidly based in the mature awareness that *true and lasting happiness* does not exist in the acquisition and manipulation of external things. I am infinitely more impressed by the person who demonstrates Spirit and has nothing, than the person who has everything, but demonstrates no Spirit. This is the extreme, for the most blessed are those that demonstrate *both*! But you get my point.

As a NexGen Human you are waking up and breaking out of this cycle of insanity. Trusting something larger, and coming to know that successful completion of the journey from Isolation-to-Integration, actually DOES result in long-term happiness.

What's new in this 21st Century Hero's Journey is the *applied* awareness that material acquisition and consumption does not result in deep joy, peace, and satisfaction. When you look closely, you'll see that these intangibles are what we are trying to buy. What we're missing and what motivates us to work so hard isn't "out there"—it's inside. As a society we've thoroughly tested the "happiness can be bought" hypothesis, and of course we keep on trying, and buying, and buying, and buying. It's time to move on and evolve! We all know the definition of insanity is doing the same thing over and over again expecting different results, but it appears that won't stop us from trying!

As a NexGen Human you are waking up and breaking out of this cycle of insanity. Trusting something larger, and coming to know that successful completion of the journey from Isolation-to-Integration, from "Poor Suffering Bastard" to "Divinely Inspired Being," actually *does* result in lasting happiness - in fact it goes far beyond happiness to deep joy, peace, and total life satisfaction. The pursuit of happiness, becomes

YOUR LIFE'S MOSAIC

I'd like you to consider that your life is like a beautiful mosaic that you create piece by piece over time – you don't know exactly what the final picture will look like, but you do know that by authentically selecting and engaging each piece, as each piece comes together, you'll end up with your own, unique, beautiful and satisfying work of art.

We tend to look at life in a linear fashion – this follows this, then this follows that, and so and so on. Think of going to school – there's kindergarten through 12th grade, then college, then a job, then marriage, then kids, then whatever – it's all very logical and linear, and can become limiting if that's your only view of life.

Looking at your life like a mosaic, or perhaps as a patchwork quilt, is a much broader view that allows a lot more freedom and creativity. It allows each piece to stand on its own - nothing necessarily has to precede it or follow it – and other pieces, many other pieces in fact, can build off of it and go in multiple directions, all within the context of the overall mosaic of your life. And sometimes you can't see the role a particular piece will play until more of the mosaic is built. As that larger picture comes into view those

previously strange pieces suddenly make sense.

With this perspective in mind, I encourage you that as you read this book you allow it to <u>unfold</u> into your awareness, and become the unique piece it is meant to be on your path, in <u>your</u> unique mosaic. No two people will experience this book in exactly the same way – as it is with all experiences in life – and if you read this book more than once, I bet you'll find that even <u>you</u> experience it differently. So I encourage you to have YOUR experience. ALLOW it to be whatever it is meant to be on YOUR path, for you, in your unique mosaic.

I have read many, many, books. And while each has provided me something on my path, no one book was "IT" for me. Certainly some were more powerful and more impactful than others, but they <u>all</u> played a role in my unique life path and in my unique life mosaic.

This book, NexGen Human, may have one key idea for you, and it may have many – there certainly are many ideas, concepts, contexts, perspectives, and frameworks presented in this book. I don't know which ones will be key pieces for you, but I encourage you to trust that there is one, at LEAST one, key idea that will make a significant difference in your life. I invite you to consider you wouldn't be reading this right now if there wasn't.

So explore, have fun, not know, and allow the unfolding of this experience in your awareness and see what it wants to become in your presence. As a NexGen Human this is a practice of discovery embraced as you build your life's mosaic.

the actual *experience* of happiness. This is the journey of a lifetime: this is the journey of our time.

You are the cutting edge of human evolution.
You are the next generation.
You are the latest link.

At the end of every chapter are a few key questions, some opportunities for action, and a short list of powerful resources related to the material in each chapter, all intended to further deepen your exploration and expand your awareness on your journey.

QUESTIONS FOR REFLECTION

- What's your current relationship with God, Universal Intelligence, Great Spirit, Source? How strong is it, how clear is it, how free and empowered are you in that relationship?
- Is there an opportunity for you to strengthen this relationship?
- To what extent do you allow peer pressure and/or fear of change keep you from growing and exploring more of who and what you are?

Opportunities for Action

- Take a deep breath and just relax and trust the process (always a good thing, especially at the beginning of any endeavor).
- Affirm now and affirm often: The greatness of my life easily unfolds.
- Of course I recommend engaging this book wholeHEARTedly.

Powerful Resources

- Book: "The Hero With a Thousand Faces," by Joseph Campbell. While this book is a bit tedious to read, it's amazing to realize the timelessness of the Hero's Journey and its existence across diverse cultures. Understanding the historical themes, guideposts, and milestones on the journey as it has been experienced through time, is quite helpful.
- Audio Program: "The Myths and Masks of God," Volume 5, Joseph Campbell Audio Collection. This audio series is the most amazing interpretation of religious symbolism I've ever heard. Joseph reveals insight after insight pointing the way to the religious experience, rather than the intellectual understanding and literal interpretation of these historical messages. Very helpful as we evolve beyond simply understanding and believing, into actually experiencing and knowing.

Chapter II

TRANSCEND & INCLUDE

It's true: 60 billion people, plus or minus some 20 Billion, have come and gone before you. They have grappled with the experience of being human, evolving through time to this moment on earth, to YOUR moment on earth.

The average life span of human beings is now approximately 70 to 80 years – what is your time on this planet all about?
What is this time all about?
What is evolving through you?

So far, it appears our time here on this planet has been about getting things, controlling things, and having pleasurable experiences. There is nothing wrong with that, it's just that these things all operate mainly from a drive for survival and leave us exhausted, and ultimately dissatisfied, from the constant running on a treadmill. Why do we need to get things, control things, and have pleasurable experiences? I propose it's because we are empty inside and we are afraid. That may be a bold statement and perhaps a bitter pill to swallow, and yet, our commitment to full self-expression (and deep joy, peace, and satisfaction) demands we take a closer look. Consider that many of us are living in fear, as a separate little shell of a human, afraid that if we don't "stock up" and have everything under control, then bad things will happen. Certainly bad things *do* happen, and sometimes even to good people, right? And if we don't watch out, *we* might be next. That's fear talking – a fear that is at the core of the human experience right now. This fear drives a collective frenzy and sense of dissatisfaction.

So what do we tend to do? What's our normal, typical reaction? We stock up and get everything under control. When the going gets tough, the tough get going, right? Then, once we've stocked up with enough stuff and feel we have everything under control, then we go after pleasurable experiences (and note that many of us don't even get to this point – i.e. workaholics and the badge of busyness). And there are a litany of pleasurable experiences we engage in - mainly for distraction and for a moment of relief from the fear that is at the root of our lives (causing us to stock up and strive for control). This is a life based on survival, speckled with moments of pleasure here and there, to make it more bearable.

The other thing to notice is these activities – getting things, controlling things, and having pleasurable experiences – are all transient. All of these things come and go, and are *outside* of you. When the thing is gone, when the experience is over, and you are left with you, what do *you* got? THAT, my friend, is the question. Most of you reading this book have probably lived enough life to experience things coming and going. Relationships, possessions, jobs, money, etc. And when things "go," what are you left with? YOU! Eventually, like the 60 billion that have come and gone before you, all things will be gone, all control will be gone, and all experiences will be over. To what extent is your life, or has your life been, about getting things, controlling things, and having pleasurable experiences?

THE SOCIAL HYPNOSIS

So where does this fear come from and how is it so many of us are run by it? To be alive as a human being here in the 21st century is to be inundated with messages about how you should live, about what you should be/do/have/believe/and experience. To be alive in the 21st Century is to be constantly barraged by fears and manipulative messages written and concocted by others interested in getting your time, attention, energy, and money … by others living in fear trying to get things, control things, and have pleasurable experiences.

You may *think* you are thinking for yourself, but you are actually only responding to a long-standing propaganda machine perpetuating a social hypnosis of the worst kind. It's mostly fear-based and needs **you** to survive. No other human being before us has suffered such a constant barrage of brainwashing messages. It's practically impossible to avoid – have you ever caught yourself singing the jingle to some commercial selling a product you couldn't give a damn about?! It's literally drilled into our heads, on both a conscious and subconscious level!

These days it seems everything is out to get us – it's always something. Global warming, diabetes, cancer, heart disease, aids, avian flu, west nile virus, hurricanes, earthquakes, tsunamis, tornadoes, terrorists, economic recessions, depressions, asteroids from space, and on, and on, and on. These messages operate on both blatant and more subtle levels. Take for example the "threat level" we each experience when we go to an airport. We are all "advised" of the security level when we travel. When I arrived at the airport for a recent trip to Los Angeles, the threat level was

Orange, which is somewhere in the middle threat-wise. The government is basically saying there is a relatively high chance something bad could happen to me on this journey. This is not exactly joy inspiring – just the name "threat level" puts me on guard and in a fear-based mode.

It's important to note that it's not the amount of information coming at us, nor is it the means by which it is coming to us, no, it's way more about the *content* of the information and messages. For the most part the media is either entertaining us with mind-numbing bullsh*t OR putting us into a state of fear, into a mode of "watch out" because "this might happen to you." So we ping-pong between states of distracted drama and pleasure, and fear-based worries and concerns. This is no way to live, yet this is the state our typical cultural conversation and our media will put you in, BECAUSE YOU PAY THEM FOR IT. You pay them with your time, your attention, your energy, and your money.

It takes a conscious, proactive decision to shift your time, attention, energy and your money, and focus it solely on what you truly desire to create and experience.

Commercials constantly sell you messages that your life could be better and that others are basically enjoying life way more than you. Of course, if you'll just buy what they have to offer, your problems will be solved and you'll enjoy life more too.

DISTRACTED AND DISCONNECTED

In a world where images change almost every second, the "real world" with its seasons and cycles operating on hourly, daily, monthly, and yearly frequencies, has just gotten too slow and boring for us. If you were to

Taking Stock

In this chapter what we are doing is "taking stock" of our current situation. It's important to take a good, honest, hard look at the truth of our situation and what's really going on.

It's so easy in our culture to just stay on the treadmill and keep doing what we've always been doing, and keep doing what everyone else is doing assuming "this is how it is" and I just gotta keep up. It's a habit and a way of being that we've been practicing for a long time – both as individuals and as a culture. But how satisfying is it? Really?

Deep down, as a NexGen Human, you know, you can just feel, there is a new way, a more satisfying way, a more fulfilling way, that is possible. Life is not about simply "getting things, controlling things, and having pleasurable experiences." These are all fine as far as they go, but after getting enough things, and trying to control everything, and having quote unquote "pleasurable experiences" – a new awareness is wanting to unfold.

Part of coming into that new awareness is coming to realize just exactly how life is running RIGHT NOW – what is really going on here? I invite you to look around, look at other people in your life, look at the newspapers, look at the television, look at your company or workplace, look at your community, and especially look at your own life and I'll bet you'll see that what is mostly going on is people trying to "get things, control things, and have pleasurable experiences."

Taking stock of where you are now, and what is really going on here, both inside and outside of you, is a critical first step on the Hero's Journey of a NexGen Human.

watch 1 hour of TV you might see as many as 1800 different images! (1 image every 2 seconds). But if you were to look out your window at the tree outside, you'd probably see only one image: that tree. In comparison, and at first glace, it appears boring. But that's only when you look with the eyes of one who does not see, it's only when you look at the natural world with the eyes of one who has been lulled into expecting the world "out there" to entertain them and meet their needs. Only when you are looking with the eyes of one who has gone essentially numb on the inside, with all attention "out there" looking for the next hit, looking for the next "thing" to entertain them. While living a relatively empty existence, essentially dead inside, we grasp and unconsciously pray for the next fix, wanting and needing that next distraction, to take away our pain. Those are the eyes that see a "boring changeless tree" when they look out the window.

And let me take this down a notch in case you're a reader who sees "a beautiful tree."

> *What I am pointing toward here*
> *is an emerging capacity for you as a NexGen Human*
> *to actually see the "dynamic, ever changing,*
> *miraculous flow and expression of life"*
> **IN ALL THINGS.**

Trees are actually easy to see in this way, and it goes far beyond simply "a beautiful tree." You "see" with your spirit, with your entire being, not just with your eyes. In addition to seeing the tree, you actually FEEL and EXPERIENCE it. It's a new dimension of presence and awareness. Unlike the TV, the video game, the movie, the computer, or the Internet, the tree is not "doing" anything, except being. To see this amazing miracle of life requires that YOU are also fully being. Or said another way, all parts of you are fully present, open, and aware. When this NexGen Human capacity is fully developed, you'll see LIFE and UNIVERSAL ENERGY in ALL things – even garbage, and yes, eventually even in the TV, video game, movie, computer and Internet. And this IS a beautiful thing.

TRANSCEND AND INCLUDE?

Let's take a moment here and further distinguish this concept of "Transcend and Include." Some of you might think it makes more sense to turn this around and say "Include and THEN transcend." And I can see how you might think that is the case.

However, to include something, you first need something to include it in – and this is why the first thing you actually do is *transcend* your current reality. You actually have a vision, or a sense, or an inspiration toward a new reality, toward a new possibility for you and your life, BEYOND THE ONE you are currently living and experiencing.

So the first thing that happens is you transcend your current reality – IN YOUR CONSCIOUSNESS – and then, over time, as this new reality and possibility becomes more clear and real for you, as you are living into and creating it, you are also INCLUDING your past in that new reality. In a sense what is happening is you are *standing on the shoulders* of your past experiences, of your consciousness up to this point in your life, and you include everything you have been and done into the new reality and awareness that is unfolding – because, in truth, everything you have been and done up to this point in time has made you who you are right now

and has facilitated whatever awareness you are now experiencing.

So in this sense, while we are transcending, or moving beyond, our current reality, we are at the same time honoring our past by including it in the new reality and experience we are now creating.

This is not normal. What most people do is try to become something new and different by *negating* what they have been and done in the past. They cannot see how what they have been and done (especially those things they do not like, or that have "been done to them") can be a part of who they now want to be, so they try to change who they are by *getting rid of* their past. As we'll see in later chapters, this common process of trying to change oneself by negating, denying, and getting rid of the past, does not work. And in fact, actually keeps the past alive and present in each moment, which then actually **impedes** our ability to transcend those states of consciousness and holds us back.

As a NexGen Human you are aware of this paradox and mechanism and as you become inspired by new visions for your life, you include all of who you've been, and all of what you've done, as you transcend those states and create your new experience of who you are and your reality.

> *Your life has a larger purpose – the evolution of your freedom*
> *to love and be loved, to express and live your deepest purpose,*
> *passions and interests.*

As a NexGen Human, you do not deny what has come before, rather, you *transcend and include*. You see beyond current circumstances (or the past) without resistance and with no need to judge the present reality, or the past, as "wrong." Quite the opposite. Your life, and that of the world, may have been, up to now, about getting things, controlling things, and having pleasurable experiences. That is fine. Now, as an emerging NexGen Human, your opportunity is to acknowledge, accept, and even embrace, what has happened and come before as the perfect path for allowing what is NOW unfolding. What's possible now is an evolution beyond those purposes, beyond those motivations, beyond those results, into the inner realm, into the realm of personal mental, emotional, physical, and spiritual evolution (or what I call "MEPS" evolution). This is what there is for you to experience and bring forward.

It's time to dig deep into the true art of living your life. Into the part of you where true meaning and inspiration reside. It's time to muster up your courage and do the thing you came here to do. It's time to rise up, transcending and including all that you are and all that you have been, to become all that you dream of. **Your life has a larger purpose** – the evolution of your freedom to love and be loved, to express your deepest purpose, passions and interests. You are not lost, you never have been, and you never will be. You are on your path and this is the next step on your journey. This is an awakening you are ready for. Everything you are has brought you to this place, here and now, ready to Transcend and Include, ready to evolve as a NexGen Human.

"You can never change things by fighting the existing reality. To change something, build a new model that makes the existing model obsolete."

-- BUCKMINSTER FULLER

QUESTIONS FOR REFLECTION

+ How much time do you spend in the typical cultural conversation? (via TV, radio, movies, newspapers, gossip, etc.). What might it be like to spend less time?

+ What things from your past do you typically resist, deny, ignore, or avoid? Is there an opportunity to transcend and include these elements from your past?

+ What vision of the future, of <u>your</u> future, inspires and excites you?

OPPORTUNITIES FOR ACTION

+ Notice how you feel during and after you engage in the typical cultural conversation (via TV, radio, movies, newspapers, gossip, etc.). Do you feel more inspired and uplifted, or fearful and depressed? Just notice.

+ Go out into nature, into a living, breathing system of life, and just *be* with it. Just walk, or sit quietly inside the living system and see if you can *feel* it, see if you can become present to the amazing life force energy pulsing through each and every thing you can see – including yourSelf.

Powerful Resources

+ Institute of Noetic Sciences (IONS): "The 2007 Shift Report: Evidence of a World Transforming." www.noetic.org. Contact the Institute of Noetic Sciences to purchase a copy of this extraordinary report. It includes four major sections profiling the dramatic transformations taking place now in our time: 1) Collapsing and Colliding Worldviews, 2) Worldview Emergence: Where Science Meets Spirit, 3) Institutional Transformation, and 4) Personal Transformation: The IONS Research Project

+ Institute of Noetic Sciences (IONS): "The 2008 Shift Report: Changing the Story of Our Future." www.noetic.org. Contact the Institute of Noetic Sciences to purchase a copy of this extraordinary report. It includes four major sections profiling the dramatic transformations taking place now in our time: 1) Evolution and Human Nature, 2) Toward a New Scientific Synthesis, 3) The Rise of Global Civil Society, and 4) Internalizing Paradigm Shift.

Both of these reports from the Institute of Noetic Sciences provide a strong foundation and evidence for the global emergence of The NexGen Human.

Chapter III

A GOOD PLACE TO START

In *The Power of Kabbalah* audio program, author Michael Moskowitz points out there are two fundamental frequencies in the Universe: chaos and fulfillment, and that chaos is the default. Meaning that until one becomes responsible and begins choosing and creating one's life, chaos is what will be experienced. It's further explained this is the difference between being proactive or reactive in life.

Another way to see this phenomenon of human experience is to explore the nature of the mind. The mind automatically focuses on what is bad, wrong, or a threat in your life. It does this because its job is survival, to keep you alive. The default of the mind, like Kabbalah says, is to chaos, is to the negative, is to what's wrong, scary, and worrisome – because these are the things it interprets as a threat to your survival, and therefore what must be focused on. Running unchecked, this **automatic** way of seeing the world completely colors your experience in life putting fear at the core with suffering as a result. The promise or carrot that the mind holds out is that happiness and fulfillment will be yours *once all these problems are solved* (note: this is equivalent to saying "I must suffer now to have happiness, sometime, in the future" – note: that future never comes, but what does come are more and more problems and suffering further perpetuating your situation).

> *As a NexGen Human you are suspicious of any*
> *promises of "happiness in the future, if you'll just sacrifice yourself*
> *now"....especially when they come from your own mind!*

Remember, the job of the mind is NOT happiness and fulfillment, its job is survival.

Now don't get me wrong, it's good to have a part of ourselves focused on survival. Thank God for that. However, the truth is, we have *already* survived. In modern life and times, the need for this survival based mechanism is **hugely** reduced. This mechanism has us focused on the problems in our life as if they are all life threatening and must be solved before peace, relaxation, and happiness (never mind joy) can be experienced. Well, news flash, there will always be "problems" in your life, and to the extent **you** allow this mechanism to run unchecked, you will rarely, if ever, experience deep peace, relaxation, and happiness. You may experience fleeting pleasure, but as we discussed in Chapter 2, that pleasure is basically an escape mechanism trying to numb the underlying fear.

> *Notice that even when your life is 99% awesome and joyous,*
> *the mind will focus on the 1% that is not,*
> *because that is the part that "it" thinks is a threat,*
> *that is a problem, that needs to be fixed,*
> *and when it is fixed <u>then</u> you will be happy.*

By focusing on this 1%, the other awesome and joyous 99% goes out of focus and your life seems miserable.

You can see this mechanism at work in the simplest of things. For example, if I were to hold up a neatly pressed and crisp large white napkin that is pristine white over 99% of it's surface with one small black spot on it – your mind would focus right in on that black spot as something that "should not be there" and automatically pass judgment making the black spot a problem. Now you are no longer present to the 99% pristine white napkin, rather the whole thing is negatively colored by this small black spot that shouldn't be there. This is what the mind tends to automatically do with our lives as well. YOUR job, as a NexGen Human, is to know this and not allow the mind to run unchecked. The practice, and this is definitely a practice done over time to develop this important skill, is to allow *awareness* of the "problems" while intentionally and proactively focusing on the positive, good things in your life (of which there are always plenty!).

And again, please don't get me wrong here. This does not mean turning the other cheek, ignoring problems and pretending they do not exist. A NexGen Human lives very much in reality, not in some Pollyanna fantasy world. The difference is, problems for a NexGen Human are held in a context of overwhelming good, and opportunity, and grace. "Problems" for the NexGen Human are opportunities to grow, transform, and reveal even more of the good that we know is at the core of all things in life, including ourselves.

FOCUS ON THE POSITIVE, ON THE CREATIVE

As a NexGen Human, *a good place to start* is to begin embracing exactly where you are as perfect for you in your life at this time. You can enact a feeling of appreciation, gratitude, and even love, for who, what, and where you are in life. You do this because it is the most powerful way to relate to *any* moment in life. Why is this the most powerful way to relate to *any* moment in life? Because doing anything else is resisting the moment (by definition if you are not embracing or allowing, you are resisting) which removes you from the present moment, puts you in a nonexistent fantasy world where the "problem" doesn't exist, into a nonexistent world where it shouldn't be, and therefore perpetuates whatever it is you are resisting.

Think of the game tug-of-war. For that game to work it requires both sides *resisting* the energy of the other. As soon as one side stops resisting – boom! – game over – there is no game. This is exactly what happens in your life. You stop playing the game (resisting) and the game is over. While resisting you have no choice, you *have to* exert a large amount of effort to try to overcome your opponent. When you stop resisting you create options. In the game of tug-of-war if you let go, your opponent will fall on their bum, and at that moment you could walk away, or you could walk over and offer a helping hand up, or any number of things since you are free from the struggle, effortful, and time-wasting game of resistance.

The second reason you begin embracing exactly where you are as perfect for you in your life at this time is because it is a very high realization, and affirmation, of the divine perfection of the Universe. When you resist where you are in your life, you are basically saying "there is something

GOOD ALL AROUND YOU

Let's take a moment and distinguish this concept of focusing on the good. You see, I'm not saying there isn't bad things happening in the world, and I'm not saying there aren't bad people in the world, and I'm not saying bad things won't happen to you. What I am saying is the more you focus on, pay attention to, and give your energy to these "bad" things in life, the more you will experience them in your life.

It's a simple law – one that we can prove to ourselves right now. Let's play a quick little game – I want you to really do this, it will take only a moment and could profoundly impact you and your life. So, first make yourself comfortable (do that right now, make yourself comfortable). Take a deep breath – in through your nose, and let it go out through your mouth. And then settle into your chair or wherever you are and just relax.

OK. Now, don't read ahead before you do this exercise. If you do, you'll ruin the insight. What I want you to do is look around the space you are in and count the number of WHITE things you see. Take about 30 seconds or so and just look around your location and count the number of things you see that are WHITE in color. Got your count? Great.

Now, focusing very carefully on this page, and *only* this page, I want you tell me how many things around you are green. Don't look around – in fact, close your eyes for a moment and see how many green things you can remember. Do that right now, close your eyes and see how many things you can remember seeing that are green. Oh, what's that? You were counting the number of white things, and you don't really remember how many green things there were? You might remember *some* things that are green in the room, but more than likely you are far more present to things that are white.

This is exactly how it works in life. The green things around you were always there, but you were not focusing on them, you were not paying attention to them, so you did not EXPERIENCE them – you did not bring them into your awareness, EVEN THOUGH THEY WERE THERE.

So in life, on your Hero's Journey as a NexGen Human, a great **practice** to engage is to focus on the good things that are present and happening in your life – and by so doing, you will be EXPERIENCING good things happening to you in your life.

What you choose to focus on makes a HUGE DIFFERENCE.

31

wrong with reality, it *should* be different than it is …. I know how it should be and this is not it." Talk about passing negative judgment on reality! Again, this is resistance to reality and will only cause struggle.

> *There is never anything wrong, no matter how it may look,*
> *there is <u>always</u> opportunity in every challenge,*
> *and in hindsight, everything is always working out.*

Let's take a closer look at this last statement: everything is *always* working out. Hasn't everything happened in your life for a reason? Hasn't it all turned out and made you who you are at this point in time? And if it looks like it hasn't "all turned out" I can practically guarantee that it will over time. So if it's true that everything is always turning out – no matter how it may look – then it's fair to say that *your life is turning out right now, and is in each and every moment.* It never is not turning out. So *relax*, trust this fact, and allow your life to just turn out!

An Attitude of Gratitude

No matter where you are in life, there is *always* something to be grateful for. As a NexGen Human you are always looking for this. This does not mean you deny, ignore, or avoid, any difficult situations, information, or circumstances. Quite the opposite.

> *Knowing there is always opportunity in every challenge,*
> *you are not afraid to embrace and*
> *acknowledge the <u>truth</u> about a situation.*

In fact, as a NexGen Human, you know the only way to find that opportunity is to accept how things actually are – not to dwell there, not

GOOD AT THE CORE

A number of years ago, when I was just beginning to coach others in their full self expression, I had a particularly resistant participant I was having a hard time connecting with and working with. It seemed he was "stuck in his life," had insurmountable problems, and that there was no way he was going to be able to do and have what he wanted in life. And he was doing a better job of convincing me of that being true than I was of convincing him that it wasn't and that there were other possibilities and options.

So, I went to my coach and explained to her the problem I was having…. and I will never forget what she told me. She said "Roger, you're speaking to the wrong part of him. He's a smart cookie, and trying to intellectually convince him of anything is never going to work and won't serve him. What you want to do is speak to that deepest part of him, speak to his SOUL. Focus on and connect with that part of him that is unlimited, that is inspired, and **wants** to play that bigger game that his mind is talking him out of. Speak to that deepest part of him and you two will blow right through that smoke screen of the mind and find amazing possibilities will open up."

So the next time I got on the phone with him, and from then on, I spoke to that deepest part of him. I visualized a golden glowing light shining forth from his body that was powerful, and inspired, and totally capable of living his dreams. I connected with that. And you know what, my coach was right, we did blow past his intellectual smoke screens and during our coaching relationship he had amazing breakthroughs and went on to fulfill his dream of supporting peace in a war torn part of Mexico, mobilizing the efforts of many and being written up in the newspaper for his efforts.

Ever since then I do this with everyone I interact with, I speak to the deepest part of them. I speak to that part of them that sees the reasons WHY, rather than the reasons why not. I speak to the SOUL that KNOWS anything is possible when divine inspiration is present.

And I encourage you to do the same with those people in your life. No matter how they may be showing up in your life, no matter what they may be saying or doing, you can always see and connect to that golden light that is in each and every one of us, IF you are looking for it (it may be a little dull and hard to see), but I guarantee, that if you start looking for it, and speaking to that part of people, that golden light will get brighter – not only in them, but in YOU as well.

to stay there and focus all the energy and attention there – but rather to courageously understand and embrace, all the while committed to moving through the challenge and unveiling the gift within. Note, the original definition of courage was "of and from the heart" – from the French root "coeur" or heart. Our society, like with so many other things, has taken the depth and heart out of the word courage so that now it's more about bravery and valor rather than a truly courageous person who makes themselves vulnerable by opening his or her heart and fully engages, embraces, and reveals their truth of a situation.

The highest realization and practice of this NexGen Human capability is to see that *Love* is at the core of absolutely everything in the Universe. No matter what disguises it may be putting on, and no matter how deep it may be buried, as a NexGen Human you know, you look for, you see, you speak to, and you inspire the love that is at the core of everything and that ultimately wants to be expressed, received, and realized in this world. To competently live this capacity of a NexGen Human, you must realize this about *yourself*, and do the work that will allow *your* love to be expressed, received, and realized in this world. And that is the topic of our next chapter.

Questions for Reflection

+ What percent of your time do you spend focusing your attention and energy on problems and negative things in your life, vs. being grateful for and focusing your energy and attention on all the great things in your life? Write down a ratio.
+ When was the last time you actually acknowledged someone for something you appreciated about them or that you were grateful

for? When was the last time you acknowledged and appreciated *yourself* – perhaps just for being you?

. In the presence of anger and fear, how peaceful and present are you able to remain? Do you allow the anger and fear of others to affect you (reactive), or can you see that it's all about them (no matter how it may look) and allow them to move through their experience while you remain calm and receptive? Note: the more reactive you are to the anger and fear of others, the more work you likely have to do to heal and release <u>your own</u> anger and fear. It's the anger and fear IN YOU that is being activated by others and this fundamentally has nothing to do with them.

Opportunities for Action

. Get out a blank sheet of paper and write down everything you are grateful for in your life. Do this until you can't think of anything else. I bet you'll be surprised at just how much great stuff there is in your life and just how much you take that for granted everyday. Notice how you feel after doing this exercise.

. Acknowledge someone in your life for something you appreciate about them – it can be anybody and it can be about anything – just your willingness to focus on the positive and share that with someone else is a powerful act in and of itself. Keep it simple and focused, it might be as simple as "I really appreciate having you in my life. Thank you." Notice how YOU feel after doing that.

. When someone is being something other than love to you in your life – they may be angry, criticizing, judging, or mean – practice "receiving their arrows of fear," internally transforming them to arrows of love, and send them back to open their heart and unveil the love you **both** want to experience.

Powerful Resources

+ Beyond Belief Audio Program: Love Expander & Ascension Accelerator. This is a powerful guided meditation and visualization that will help you focus your attention and energy on the power of love and gratitude in your life. All Beyond Belief audio programs are: 1) designed with busy lives in mind – this program takes less than 15 minutes, 2) include a deep relaxation process which reduces stress, feels great, and puts you in a receptive, creative state, and 3) involve YOU – they are "a container or framework inside of which YOU show up," therefore they are naturally customized to you and grow with you each time you use them. As one person who uses this program has said "This is the Buddah's loving kindness meditation brought into the modern age." Visit www.GoBeyondBelief.com/products.php to purchase this program.

+ Beyond Belief Audio Program: Shift It – Accessing the Gift Within. This is a powerful guided meditation and visualization designed to transform blocks, challenges, and issues into opportunities. It uses the energy and intelligence of your higher self to reveal the gift within each problem, challenge, or block. By using this program you are training yourself to access your higher power and self whenever you face a challenge or difficult situation. It is designed with busy lives in mind and can be completed in less than 20 minutes. As one person who uses this program has said "Shift It helps me tremendously whenever I feel stuck or overwhelmed. It's totally amazing to me how well this works." Visit www.GoBeyondBelief.com/products.php to purchase this program.

Chapter IV

The Great Transformation

OK. Now, here is where much of the heavy lifting is done when it comes to evolving into a NexGen Human. Some of the language I use in this chapter may be a bit abrasive – I apologize in advance for that – but I want to "get in your face" a bit about this particular aspect of powerful living and evolution. If some of your buttons are pressed while reading this chapter I want you to celebrate that. When your buttons are pressed know that these are red flags representing valuable opportunities for transformation and growth in *your* life. No matter how it may look, and how justified you may feel, where *your* buttons get pressed are places in *your* life where you are holding yourself prisoner. The key is to witness or observe *your* reactions and note the area(s) you are resisting. These areas are opportunities for increased freedom and expression of your Self – in other words "there is gold to be mined" in those areas of your life. OK, enough of the preamble. Here we go.

> *The Great Transformation of our time*
> *is the transformation of the individual*
> *from victim to creator.*

"Yeah right," you might say. Or: "What? Me? A victim?"

If either of these is your first response to this statement, know that it is completely normal. In fact, skepticism and incredulous disbelief are the automatic first stage of developing this awareness and NexGen Human trait. This transformation cannot be underestimated for both its importance and its challenge; the initial realization can be quite a jolt. As a NexGen Human, however, you will make this great transformation in your life.

The importance of this shift is in the act of reclaiming personal power. As long as you are a victim, in *any* area of your life, your power remains in the hands of others; other people, other systems, other institutions, other anything. As long as you remain a victim of whatever you claim to be victimized by, you remain powerless to effect change and create your life the way you truly want it. Ironically and paradoxically, you are both the prisoner <u>and</u> the jailer…YOU hold the keys to the freedom you so desire. Again, the importance of this transformation cannot be underestimated. Until you cross this threshold of evolution, you will be stuck, and suffering, unable to move forward and create the life you truly desire.

"Our power comes the day we recognize we are not limited by outer world circumstances and situations."
- JOHN KEHOE, BEST SELLING AUTHOR OF "MIND POWER"

Who Did This To Me and How Did It Happen?

Believe it or not, there actually ARE some perpetrators. Other people actually did do some things to you and you reacted and interpreted those actions in the way that you did. Whether you attracted those actions into your life and whether they were good or bad is a conversation for another book. For now, let's just stick to the simple fact that "something happened to you" and you "interpreted" it in the way that you did (likely as something bad and wrong that should not have happened) and you reacted (and likely continue to react) based on that original interpretation (likely made when you were very young).

With this as background, some of the perpetrators are obvious ones. For example, your parents. It's easy to blame one or both of your parents for any problems you might be having in your life. And the funny thing is, you're probably right. I don't know anybody who wasn't wounded in some way shape or form as a child – it's just part of growing up. Everyone is wounded in childhood, including even <u>your parents</u>. In fact, if they hadn't been wounded in the way they were by THEIR parents, they wouldn't have passed that on to you in the way that they did.

Mythological stories about "the great wounding" reveal the natural role of parents as the ones who cause harm, whether they want to assume that role or not. From an archetypal perspective, it's normal and natural for a parent to inflict some kind of wound on the child that causes a fall from innocence, and, in turn, initiates the Hero's Journey. On this Hero's Journey it is the job of the child – through his or her unique life path – to heal this wound and perform a kind of "alchemy" that transforms pain into love. Seen in this light, your wounds are your divine destiny, for they provide your greatest challenge and opportunity: to heal yourself and create freedom and Love *by your own choice.*

Another way to look at this childhood wounding is to notice that we've all had traumatic experiences while growing up. Then notice that being righteous about what happened to you while growing up, and blaming the people who did it to you, is not going to change your situation. I repeat – that is NOT going to change your situation. Has it yet? What WILL change your situation is to stop being a victim of whatever happened to you, recognize that everyone is always doing the best they can given the knowledge they had at the time, their circumstances, challenges, *consciousness,* and the fears and survival drivers THEY were living with in their own lives at that time …. and FORGIVE them (and yourself).

One very important thing to notice is that forgiveness is more about YOU and YOUR experience, than it is about the other person. Holding a grudge makes YOU miserable, **not** the other person. And while the other person may feel a little better knowing that you have forgiven them (if they ever even know), the person benefitting the most will be YOU.

You hold the antidote to the poison you have taken.

I recommend you give it to yourself as soon as possible, put yourSelf in the drivers seat, and step onto your *creative* path.

Now, believe me, I know what a challenge this can be. And depending on where you are in your life, and perhaps how much pain you have suffered, it can take a long time to fully engage this level of forgiveness and responsibility in your life. Also, it's typically easier to transform something if you have suffered much pain. Why? Because the cost – pain

– eventually outweighs the benefit – righteousness. It's just too painful to maintain your way of being. When one is initially waking up to the victim role they've been playing in their life, it's typically through the path of pain and suffering. This was true for me. If all were "fine and dandy" there would be far less motivation to seek new understanding, awareness, and experience. So in this light, the pain is good, and you can actually ride it or leverage it, to higher consciousness, new experiences, and ways of being in your life.

Your Life is On Automatic – Until it Isn't

On the path of evolution, "The Great Transformation"—from powerless victim to responsible creator—is the first MAJOR transformation that happens for people. It is literally an evolutionary advance that wants to happen at a certain stage of human development. This is the "rub" in the popular movie *The Secret*, which points out that YOU are the creator of your life. You create it ALL—the good AND the bad. That can be a tough pill to swallow, because you must become responsible for your life (or as I like to say response-able). When you awaken to this realization you can no longer play victim and blame others for your failures and misery – you *realize* you are creating it, ALL of it.

Now this is both good news and bad news. The good news is you do not have to be a victim, YOU can do something about it. And the bad news is YOU have to do something about it. You cannot wait around for someone else to come along and fix your life for you. It's really up to you. Stop for a moment and say out loud: My life is up to me. Go ahead say it and see how it feels.

My life is up to me.

41

Let this soak in a bit. I bet you'll find it feels really good to climb into the drivers seat, perhaps a bit scary, but good-scary. This is where you start reclaiming your personal power.

Up until this moment, in whatever area of life you've been playing a victim, you've been giving your personal power to that *thing* that has had control of you, that has had *more power* than you.

> *The Great Transformation is the awakening*
> *that marks the beginning of the end*
> *for you as a victim.*

Part of the awakening here is simply growing up and becoming an adult in those areas of our lives where we are still children. You see, when we were children we actually WERE victims – so it's not that this story we believed was *never* true – the way we experienced the world was the way we experienced the world. It was true at one point in our life and we got very pissed-off about that. However, I'm sure you can see it was from a very *limited* view of the world. When you are 6, or 7, or 8 years old, you haven't seen much of the world, nor have you interacted with very many of the people in it. You only knew what you were exposed to and that was it. However, over the years, as we develop adult competencies, distinctions, and capacities, we become far more able to take responsibility for our lives. We develop a far larger *context* inside of which our life is happening. And eventually the opportunity arrives when we can actually choose to be responsible about how we are reacting to our hurts, our trials and tribulations as a child, and CHOOSE IN THIS MOMENT, AS AN ADULT, how we are going to relate to and perceive those incidences in our lives that hurt us – we can continue to make people wrong (and continue our personal suffering as a victim) OR transcend and include. Perhaps THIS is just such a moment for you.

Uncovering Your Layers of Victim

At more advanced levels of this competency (being responsible as the creator of everything you experience in your life), deeper and more subtle stories of playing victim come to light. For example, people love to blame the government, the economy, the weather, their spouse, their kids, their finances, their health, and on, and on, and on! In all of these circumstances there is choice. Choice to be responsible for your life and the events in it, or the choice to be a victim and not responsible for the events in your life.

Choosing to be a victim may be easy and feel good in the moment –
you get to be right, blame others for your miserable circumstances,
and then do nothing about it –
but in the long run it is very painful.

If you have not already made this transformation in your life, and if you are like me, it will take a fair amount of built up pain until you change. At that point, the cost of being a victim FAR OUTWEIGHS the short lived, in the moment, benefits of playing the victim. The built up pain provides a sling-shot like effect that propels you out of the pain and into acceptance. It just hurts too much and takes too much energy to keep holding the grudge, so you surrender to the healing and forgive.

It's important to point out that while this transformation may happen initially as a huge AHA! moment of new insight awareness and freedom, it continues throughout life. Taking responsibility for ALL areas of your

THE POWER OF PAIN

I want to provide a couple of examples for how pain and suffering can be very helpful and motivating on our evolutionary path. Transformation can happen as a result of many things, it does not have to be the result of pain and suffering, however some of my most powerful moments of transformation were preceded by, and instigated by, a period of pain and suffering.

If you are experiencing pain and suffering in your life right now, and I'm talking mostly in the mental and emotional realms, although those certainly can and often do manifest physically as well....but if you are experiencing pain and suffering right now in one or many parts of your life, know that this is likely a sign of new things to come. When you get sick and tired of being sick and tired, the energy for transformation becomes quite high. Let me give you a couple of examples.

Many years ago I was experiencing a mild level of depression in my life. I just wasn't happy anymore, I didn't have any enthusiasm for life, I was just plodding along feeling like crap most of my days, and pasting it over the best that I could doing what I simply had to do to survive. I knew there was more to life, and I wanted to be there and experience that, but I just couldn't access it and I didn't know how.

A few months prior to this stage in my life a friend had sent me a letter after participating in a training program that made a big difference in her life and in that letter she was urging me to check it out. Well, that letter sat on my desk for at least three months while I thought to myself "that's nice for her, maybe I'll check it out someday, I'll keep it here for future reference." Now in this moment of mild depression that letter came to the forefront of my awareness and as I re-read it I thought to myself, "what do I have to lose" and I put myself in that program that turned out to be exactly what I needed at that time in my life.

What I want you to notice here is the PATH and PROCESS of transformation. I was feeling down and depressed and had come to a place where I was OPEN to new things – what I had been doing up until that point obviously was *no longer* working. From that place of awareness and openness I had enough energy and willingness to try something new, and put myself in a program that a friend recommended. I never would have done that had my pain and suffering not spurred me to expand my horizons.

Here's another example. As I was engaging a path of wealth-building and success I experienced much frustration. Talk about a path of trial and error! At one point I was so frustrated and angry and confused – since everything I was trying was not working out – that I decided to hire a therapist and go deep, one on one, into the patterns that were running my life. I did some research and trusted my intuition as to who to hire and work with and I'll never forget one of first things my therapist said to me after listening to me describe my situation, he said "Roger, your mind is in WAYYYY over it's head" – that resonated so true for me in my experience. I worked with this therapist for 9 months seeing him for 2 hours each week and healed parts of myself that I don't know how I would have without that professional partnership.

The point is, once again, I had come to a place of pain and suffering, manifesting as frustration and anger – that provided me the energy and motivation to seek something new and explore new realms. What I was doing was no longer working, it was not producing the results and life experience I desired, so I opened up to new things.

As much as we hate it, as much as we resist it, as much as we try to avoid it, what I have found is that pain and suffering can be a great transformational motivator and are signs that new ways of living and new possibilities for your life are wanting to be born.

life is an ongoing endeavor. Besides the fact that the external world and circumstances are <u>very</u> convincing, it's just too easy to play victim and *believe* in our own supposed personal limitations, e.g. I'm not smart enough, good enough, motivated enough, etc., etc. These are all victim stories we tell ourselves, that keep us powerless, stuck, and going in circles.

"Most people are extras in their own movie."

- BRIAN TRACY

Questions for Reflection

+ Are there areas in your life where you can stop being a victim and become more response-able? What and where might these areas be?

+ Are there people in your life YOU can benefit from forgiving? Who might they be?

+ How much pain and suffering have you created from being a victim or holding a grudge in your life? Think how great it would feel FOR YOU to let that go.

Opportunities for Action

+ If you were to focus on one of those areas from the first question above and become less of a victim and more like a responsible creator, what might that look like? What would be your first step or action? Take it.

+ Take a person from your list in the second question above and mentally forgive that person RIGHT NOW. Feel how good the forgiveness feels FOR YOU. Write them a letter, give them a call, or visit them in person to let them know you have forgiven them (and perhaps that you love them).

Powerful Resources

If you are really stuck in victim mode and struggling to make this transition, I highly recommend Landmark Education Corporation's three day training program called *The Forum*. This is the best program I have ever experienced for putting your past into the past and becoming free and responsible for your life in the present moment. It is the evolution of Werner Erhard's *est* training. I never experienced *est*, but the people I have met who have (and I've met quite a few) have all said it was a phenomenal training that went beyond words to describe it. *The Forum*, while challenging and controversial to some, is an amazing value for what it offers (freedom from your past and the stories you keep on telling yourself and everyone else). Some people feel their "sales model" is too aggressive. I suggest you notice what presses your buttons and begin owning your own perspectives and know that you ALWAYS have the power to choose for yourself – i.e. no one can *make* you do anything. Visit www.LandmarkEducation.com to register for a program near you.

Chapter V

It's All About Evolution

So after this Great Transformation what's next? What's next is evolution. Actually the Great Transformation is itself an act of incredible evolution, so what's really next is *ongoing* evolution. This is where the rubber meets the road so to speak. This is when you start to get some traction in your life and your car actually starts moving forward (as a creator), rather than going around and around in circles (as a victim). After making the Great Transformation and putting yourself in the driver's seat of your life, what's next is navigating your *creative* process(es).

It's important to note that evolution happens *in the gap* between your present reality and your desired reality. This can be called the creative gap or transformational gap. You create this gap when you state, embrace, and define your dream(s) and/or something you want to experience in life. Without a sizable gap, not much evolution will be happening. You know the story ... you're comfortably uncomfortable, you're just cruising along, and more than likely you're bored but too lazy to do anything about it. In that place, not much evolution and growth is going to happen. Note, however, that it's perfectly fine to plateau for awhile, as life has natural cycles. For a NexGen Human, plateaus are natural resting places of transition where you enjoy the fruits of past labors and/or wait for divine inspiration and the next creative endeavor to become more clear. The point is: you evolve, grow, and expand <u>in the gap</u>; without a sizable gap there ain't much evolving, growing, and expanding going on.

Navigating your creative processes involves evolving all aspects of yourself (Mental, Emotional, Physical, and Spiritual – or "MEPS" evolution) to bigger and bigger levels. This process never ends. For every transformation and expansion you create and experience, there is another waiting right around the corner. This is the path, this is the process, this is your opportunity.

As a NexGen Human, it is your profound opportunity and privilege to consciously, and responsibly, participate in your own evolution, to wider and wider experiences of freedom and deeper and deeper experiences of Love.

The freedom you can create is limitless, and the depth of love you can experience is also without limit. Wow. Now that is an amazing gift and opportunity, yes?

The "Hard Work" of Today

The hard work of today is not so much the hard work of industrial age lore of "making things happen" (think bulldozer metaphor of manipulating and pushing things around expending a tremendous amount of energy and force).

The hard and courageous work of today is INNER WORLD WORK – healing your OWN wounds, integrating and welcoming ALL aspects of yourself and becoming a self-realized, whole and complete, free, loving and present being.

In the Industrial Age model the goal, the dream, was material success, at pretty much any cost – the underlying assumption being "if I am rich and powerful, I will be happy." We now know this is not necessarily true. To know how well we are doing in today's important work we need to ask ourselves new and different questions. Ask yourself the following questions to get a sense of your transformational opportunity:

+ How free am I? In <u>all</u> areas of my life.
+ How joyful am I?
+ How loving am I?
+ How much love do I experience each day?
+ How peaceful am I in my life?
+ How present, in each moment, am I?
+ How much awe and beauty do I experience each day?
+ Am I fulfilling the highest vision of my life?

The work of today, of the NexGen Human, is to become that stillpoint at the center of all creation, with complete and total freedom to move in any truly authentic and Source inspired direction. As you do THIS *hard work* the other hard work of "getting things done" (bulldozer) gets easier and easier.

Getting Yourself Out of the Way

So this *work* is all mostly a process of "getting yourself out of the way." This is your self with a small "s". Life force energy, big "S" Self, wants to flow through you but *we* tend to block it up with resistance, dis-belief, and fears of all kinds – from large to small.

Life Force Flow

BLOCKS: "Beliefs" like – "It's not possible", "I'm not worthy", "I'm not lovable," "I'm incompetent," "I don't matter," "It's not worth it," "It's too hard," etc., etc., etc.

For many people, most, if not all, of their actions in life are rooted in a fear of some kind. As we saw in the first two chapters, fear is running rampant in our society. As a NexGen Human, you are aware of this, and you are now on the path of transforming *your* life, and evolving, such that your life is rooted in Love.

Personal evolution is a process of embracing,
allowing, and thereby transcending your fears.
You come to a place where you have fears,
instead of your fears having you.

Depending on how much internal growth and transformation you have already experienced in your life, as well as the nature of your life in general, you may have a lot of work to do in this area. On the other hand, if you have done a lot of work in this area already, you may have more of a "maintenance" amount of work to do. I say maintenance because no matter how many fears you transcend, fears will never go away. They are part of the wiring of human being, it's a survival thing, and its part of our biological evolution. In fact, as stated in *The 2007 Shift Report – Evidence of a World Transforming* published by The Institute of Noetic Sciences, the human brain has more than doubled in size over the past 1.9 million years:

> "*The development of our frontal lobes has made us better able to anticipate the future, keep our impulses in check, set goals, and avoid dangers. But these same lobes are also a major source of neurotic thoughts and behaviors. They enable us to worry – Did I lock the door? Did I say the right thing? Will I find a job? Will I ever get married? – and increase our capacity to acknowledge our own mortality – Will I get cancer? How will I care for my family? The frontal lobes provide steady work for mental health professionals.*"

Fears are typically rooted in the past, projected into the future, and hijack your life in the present. We are unique on this planet in our ability to do this – to live in the past and future – however, it's not an enjoyable way to live. Our drive for survival is on automatic and "life just turns out this way." That's fine when you are growing up. But as a NexGen Human you have *already* survived, and are now evolving beyond survival – transcending, but still including it (don't' worry, your drive for survival will always be there, it's just no longer going to be the root cause of your experience and actions). You do this by becoming aware of all the areas in your life, all the thoughts and feelings you are having, and actions you are taking (all of them), and questioning their source – are they coming from fear or love? If you notice a thought and feeling and identify its source as fear, celebrate! That is a huge moment of transformation.

The fears at the root of your thoughts, feelings, and actions are transformed in a string of moments wherein you <u>see</u> the root fear and choose differently. Instead of unconsciously coming from fear, you consciously choose to trust and come from a place of Love. This is transformation.

As with pretty much any new skill you learn, this will not be easy in the beginning, especially with long standing beliefs and perceptions of the world. Be compassionate with yourself and be persistent. The more you *observe* your thoughts, feelings, and actions, the more you *have them*, vs. *them having you*. Just the mere act of observation puts you in a mode that is no longer *identified* with the thoughts, feelings, and actions. From this place of observation, you have more freedom and more options.

Fears are actually great signs of transformational opportunity. You see, the truth is that we are amazingly powerful, creative beings that can overcome any situation that may ever present itself (history is FULL of these kinds of stories) – but we don't believe this, especially about ourselves – hence the fears. Fears actually are signs there is a part of you that is out of alignment with the truth of who you really are. In this

THE SOCIAL MASK

There are two messages it's important to appreciate in this chapter: 1) everyone is working through their own challenges even though it doesn't look like it, and 2) it's the rare and unusual human being that can competently help you heal your wounds and move you along your evolutionary path.

As a NexGen Human, don't be fooled by the Social Mask. Life is messy, and everyone is working through their own challenges – but it doesn't *look* this way – people hide that part, and put on the image, put on their smile, put on their *social mask* as it is known. To know this is true, just look at your own life. I bet you do this yourself, I know I do. And it's not that this isn't appropriate. In social situations the grand majority of people are not equipped or have any idea how to support your healing, so to drop your social mask and bear your "ugly wounds" would end up, more than likely, alienating others and leaving your wounds gaping even larger. We intuitively know this, so we don't do it.

It takes a person who has healed their own wounds, and can meet your pain with compassion and understanding, to support you through it. In many cultures, this is the role of the wise elder. If you have a wise elder in your life, consider yourself blessed. However, since most people have not done their own work, when you share your hurts with the average person out there, it only activates theirs, and puts them into a judgment and rejection mode – or some kind of a sympathy or fixing mode – which again, leaves you more than likely worse off than when you started!

Now again, note that this is good to a certain extent; none of us wants to hear a bunch of dumping and complaining from others. But it's also important to note that this is what people usually do – they dump and complain.

On the other hand, responsible sharing, the kind that a NexGen Human would do, where you own your own stuff with an authentic desire for healing AND an openness to coaching and insight, is much less frequent.

Many, and I would say perhaps even most, adults have avoided this kind of responsible, authentic, and courageous sharing. Why? Because 1) it's not painful enough, at least consciously, for them to deal with, 2) initially it's much easier to stuff it down, paste it over, and pretend that everything is OK, 3) they have no structure or model for this kind of conversation, 4) they fear being vulnerable in this way will somehow hurt them and make them less powerful, and 5) they have no one in their life that can actually help them heal their wounds and evolve into more freedom and love. Therefore, these people are walking bundles of reactionary protection mechanisms and patterns from their past that they continue to keep alive each and every present moment. And these are the average people you are likely to be surrounded by as you engage with what we call "the general public."

So just be aware of the environment you are walking in. Be aware that your fellow human beings are all working through their own issues, even though it does not look like it, be aware of who you are sharing with and recognize the limitations the average person

will have in helping you with your wounds and your healing process, and be responsible for your own issues – sharing authentically with a true desire for healing and support – and then, perhaps you can become the one who listens compassionately and helps others heal their own wounds.

Note, this is also the role that good therapists and counselors play in society. My company Beyond Belief has assembled a list of excellent, spiritually-based therapists and counselors who can facilitate the powerful healing so many in our society will benefit from. When it comes to deep healing and transformation, there is no substitute for a 1-on-1, personalized, professional process engaged over time.

context, fears then become markers indicating you're on your path of evolution and expansion. They tell you that you're moving in the right direction. In fact, it could be said that to really maximize your evolution and expansion, you want to always be moving in the direction of what you are afraid of, since these are areas where you have the most illusion and dis-belief in yourself. These are your greatest opportunities for transformation and expansion.

The antidote for fear is action.

Most people *believe* their fears and therefore get caught up in their tangled web. This then leads to all sorts of pain, suffering, and contracted actions. The normal way of dealing with fears is to avoid, deny, and pretend they don't exist, or incessantly fret over them. None of these are effective actions. They just keep the fear in place – as if it is real – and debilitate us in the process. The opportunity for a NexGen Human is to change the context of fears. You can change the context from the normal and reactionary "oh no, bad things are going to happen to me" – to "Oh, I see I'm having a fear-based thought, this is an area where I can experience great transformation and expansion."

Your Mind Can Change Your Brain

One of the most exciting aspects of doing this work is that you are literally changing your physiology. Beliefs, habits, and old ways of perceiving the world are not just invisible ideas made up in the mind, they are imprinted patterns that literally exist in your physiology. This is both a good thing and a bad thing. It's good because once we learn something, it tends to stay with us – we don't have to *think about* how to tie our shoes, drive a car, brush our teeth, or any number of things we do each and every day. We have imprinted our physiology to automatically do these things. However, the "bad" old habits and beliefs that no longer serve us run on automatic too! And it's these old patterns, habits, and beliefs we want to transform and evolve beyond. These are the parts of ourselves that are now holding us back from the freedom, success, love, happiness, and power we desire.

> *"The number one reason people don't achieve or hold on to new success, is they haven't released old issues."*
> - LISA NICHOLS, BEST SELLING AUTHOR, COACH AND SPEAKER

Science is now discovering "How the Brain Rewires Itself." An excellent article by that title ran in *Time Magazine* on January 19, 2007 that summarized and highlighted some of the most important studies in this arena. Amazingly, these studies are revealing that "mental training has the ability to change the physical structure of the brain." And these aren't fringe, quack scientists performing this work. These studies are being done by neuroscientists at leading institutions like Harvard Medical School, The University of California San Diego, The University of California Los Angeles, The University of Toronto, and The University of Wisconsin at Madison.

These studies reveal how "The brain can change as a result of the thoughts we think…something as seemingly insubstantial as a thought can affect the stuff of the brain, altering neuronal connections in a way that can treat mental illness, or, perhaps, lead to a greater capacity for empathy and compassion. It may even dial up the supposedly happiness set point." The researchers are calling this newly discovered capacity of the brain *neuroplasticity*. This is very important news for a NexGen Human, because what this says is that by practicing desired (chosen) thoughts, feelings, and actions, we can literally rewire ourselves to experience (and create) the world as we now desire. Through "self directed neuroplasticity, the mind can change the brain." We are not, as was long believed, prisoners of our DNA, genetics, or childhood conditioning. While it will take some discipline and it will occur over time, it's exciting to know you have a choice! You can literally change your physiology and sculpt your experience of reality.

Transcending Your Fears

So let's take a look at how this transformation of our physiology might take place. Let's investigate what that path might look like. First, let's notice that the old habits, patterns, and beliefs that would be good to transform are mostly rooted in fears of some kind. And the level to which fear is rooted in our society is alarming – however, as a result, the opportunity to create real freedom, and the opportunity to experience greater depths of Love, is also truly amazing! That's what you get as you do this work – more trust, more freedom, and more Love. As a NexGen Human consciously participating and walking your path of Evolution, what you are creating for yourself, and for others, is the authentic experience of wider and wider freedom and deeper and deeper Love. Of the many things in life one can create and experience, I think freedom and Love rank pretty high!

When you are coming from fear, when you are gripped by fear, by definition you are not free, and you are certainly not experiencing Love.

As a NexGen Human you are done with the fear thing. You are done letting fear run your life. You are done struggling to survive and you commit to questioning every fear in your life. You become motivated and authentically inspired by your desire to experience more *love and freedom* in your life. Notice I did not say resisting your fears – this is a very important distinction. Resistance causes persistence (remember the tug-of-war example?) – if you want to release your fears, stop resisting them. And instead, allow them. With nothing for them to push against they fall away.

This is a paradox the mind does not understand – it does not make *logical* sense to the mind that embracing and allowing something is the path to its release – the mind *thinks* embracing and allowing will create MORE of what it does not want, hence it continues to resist…which ironically causes the persistence. More on all this in a moment.

Let's take a look at where fears may be lurking in our lives. Here's a list of BIG fears. See if any of these may be present in your life:

- Death
- Losing your job, or financial income
- Loss of a loved one – child, spouse, family member, friend
- Judgment or rejection from others, for any reason
- Letting others down, disappointing others
- Losing your home or "being on the streets"
- Failing at some aspect of your life – a work project or business endeavor, relationships, etc.
- Losing your health, becoming disabled in some way, or suffering some kind of physical pain
- Being robbed, beaten, shot, stabbed, or abused in some way
- Hurting others

These are some of the bigger ones. And in looking at them they are a little scary, yes? However, this is the point. You want to start *really looking* at these. To the extent they lie lurking in the background, unacknowledged yet driving your thoughts, feelings, and actions, *they have you*. But as soon as you start to really look at them, and *question them*, they start losing their grip. And once they start losing their grip, you can continue to see through them, let them go, and begin to replace them with creative and inspirational sources for action.

Someone once said "To be truly free, you must die while still alive." It's a paradox of life that to be free of something undesirable, you must embrace it. This doesn't mean you have to become homeless, or lose your job, or literally die. What it means is you *embrace it* mentally and emotionally, and no longer resist or avoid it! Where do you think these

Discovering Your SLBs

I want to provide a real world example from my life for how the discovery, or making conscious, your Subconscious Limiting Beliefs (SLBs) might go.

One SLB I had running in my life showed up like this: I am fully expressing myself and giving of myself from a pure and loving place when suddenly something happens and I am rejected or negatively judged or put down in some way. My first and fully automatic reaction is shock, since I cannot believe this has happened. It makes no sense to me why someone would shut me down and reject me so harshly when I am sharing from a pure and loving place. After the shock, comes hurt, which then pretty quickly turns to anger. I get pissed off at this person or people for doing this to me, and then after the anger I go into a mode of rejection. I "take my marbles and go home" and reject and scorn them and play "an eye for an eye."

This belief system, and automatic way of being, arose from experiences in my childhood. I would bet that almost every child has an experience like this of some kind, somewhere while they are growing up, where they are being the free spirited child they are, and someone – whether another child or an adult – criticizes them, tells them to stop, or even angrily shuts them down (the most common word a child hears while growing up is NO). If you think about it, in society, the fear of rejection, or failure, or of public humiliation is very common and very high. Have you ever stopped to think about where this fear comes from? In fact, I would go so far as to say that this common childhood experience, that lays down the belief that *if I trust and allow myself to freely express who I am, the world will reject me and shut me down – and that hurts*, teaches us at a very early age to *shut ourselves down* and to *not trust ourselves* and to *be very careful about what we say and do*, and to *protect our hearts* because we know from past experience that letting ourselves go, from that pure and loving place, can result in criticism, rejection, and even anger from others … and that really hurts.

Another thing to notice is the powerful effect of a negative experience vs. a positive one. While the mind may remember good times, what the mind will NEVER forget is a bad time. While a child may receive many words and expressions of love and encouragement, it takes only one intensely negative experience for the psyche of that child to be changed forever. Just look in your own life. Don't we tend to slough off all the positive comments? But as soon as one, and only one, negative comment shows up in our space, whoa, watch out, we become very sensitive. Even if it's only one percent of our feedback, that's what we focus on. That's the job of the mind, it's the sentry, always watching for danger and guarding against it happening again.

So it's easy to see how this limiting belief could be running, subconsciously for the most part, in almost everyone in society! And this one belief will stop you in your tracks - you do not want, and your mind will not allow - you to experience that hurt again. It hurt so much you just won't go there again. It's far safer to shut down your heart, play it safe, be angry at the world that they will not embrace and love you, and take your gifts to your grave!

This is why people shake on stage, why we avoid our passions, why we toil in places and jobs we don't love, why we don't do most of what is near and dear to our hearts *because* we already tried that and it only led to hurt, so we ain't doing it again. This is the core of the Hero's Path – this is the path of the NexGen Human – it's a path of healing, freeing yourself from your own Subconscious Limiting Beliefs, and eventually getting your gifts out to the world in the way they are meant to be given.

fears are living for you? Even if you have actually experienced one or some of these undesirables along the way, they currently exist only in mental and emotional realms, in your thoughts and feelings. However, even as non-physical mental and emotional *memories*, they do exist in your life. To be free of these fears then, to embrace and release them, you must go where they currently exist – in your own mental and emotional realms. And, if you are right now experiencing in your physical reality, one or more of these things in your life, this is also what you do – fully embrace it! And from there, new options will begin to unfold. This is the beginning, and access to, expanded freedom and love.

A simple way I have discovered for embracing and releasing *fears of something bad happening* (in the future) is to complete the following sentence:

"While I do not prefer (to be, have, or experience)

_____*, I am not afraid."*

The first thing to do is just write down your fears and put into the blank whatever shows up in your mind. It's already there, so do not resist it. At one point when I was gripped by fear and hooked on all my worries and concerns, I did this exercise and experienced an amazing amount of relief and freedom. One of the keys to this sentence structure is that it releases your resistance to whatever you are fearing, but does not encourage it's creation – you state very clearly "While I do not prefer…." So you don't prefer to experience this thing (in physical reality), but if it is meant to be, you are not afraid, you will welcome and embrace what is meant to be. It's an interesting balance between creation and surrender – you are 1) stating your preference, 2) creating your stand of *not afraid*, and 3) surrendering, or allowing, a larger plan or way.

When I first did this exercise my statements looked like this:

- While I do not prefer to be homeless, I am not afraid.
- While I do not prefer financial failure, I am not afraid.
- While I do not prefer to be publicly humiliated, rejected, criticized, and scorned, I am not afraid.
- While I do not prefer to suffer and toil in work that does not inspire me, I am not afraid.
- While I do not prefer to be physically disabled and in pain, I am not afraid.

Then at the end you can add: "I courageously embrace ALL of life's experiences."

Overall this is a *truth telling* exercise, and telling the truth is *always* liberating (the only reason you wouldn't tell the truth is because you FEAR something, therefore telling the truth literally liberates you from that fear). So in this exercise we are embracing *our worst fears*, we are giving them some *air time* and therefore taking some of the charge off them. We stop resisting them, we stop "fearing" embracing them, we stop pushing them away "in fear" that they might come about if we acknowledge them. When you can embrace your fears you are well on your way to true liberation and freedom.

"F-E-A-R: Forgetting – Everything's – All – Right"

Let's take a simple example: fear of losing your job. If you are waking up everyday and going to work from a place of "if I don't wake up and go to work, I will lose my job," as reasonable as that may seem, it's a fear based action. You are doing it because you are afraid! Afraid of losing your job. Now use the statement "While I do not prefer to lose my job, I am not afraid." Can you feel the courage built into this statement? There is a power that is activated by this statement that "no matter what happens" you will be OK, you are not afraid.

Now you can go a little deeper into this fear and ask yourself, "What if I did lose my job?" And start to mentally and emotionally *embrace* this possibility of losing your job. What would you do next? You'd probably find another job! And it might even be a better one! Almost everyone I know who has gotten fired, laid off, or quit for whatever reason, has landed in a better place (and yes, typically after a short period of fear, worry, struggle, and concern). This has definitely been true for me. It may have taken a few months, but in the end their situation is even better! If you trusted this for yourself, you could be free of your fear of losing your job. That changes everything! Now you don't wake up and get out of bed because "if you didn't you would lose your job." You are no longer *afraid* of losing your job. Now you are going to get out of bed and go to work for a different reason. Having embraced and let go of your fear-based motivation, you can replace it with a love-based, or creative-based, motivation or inspiration. Perhaps you'll get out of bed and go to work because you appreciate the financial support it provides you in your life. This is a BIG shift. Now you are going to work *creating* financial support in your life. That feels good, and has you in the place of responsible creator, rather than in the position of fearful victim.

One other side note on this exercise of embracing your fears – let's say you do the exercise and realize YOU ARE afraid of whatever is gripping you, and that ain't changing. In this instance it's perfectly fine to simply embrace and allow your fear. You might use this sentence structure: "While it's true that in this moment I am afraid of _____ _____, I embrace and allow my fear." This is another statement of *non-resistance*. You gain power by surrendering to the truth of your experience and allowing it!

Human beings love the excitement of varied and challenging experiences; few of us would be satisfied with a boring, simple life that involves none of the pain involved in growing. We may think that what we want is to avoid challenges, pain, and suffering, but what we actually want is the POWER TO BE WITH whatever may come—*including* great challenge, pain, and suffering. Take a look for yourself right now. What do you REALLY want—no pain, suffering, or challenge? Or the power to *be with* whatever may come? Connect with your heart and look deeply—which position resonates as the more powerful place to be? What resonates as a life well lived? What resonates more as the truth of the path rather than a hopeful fantasy? I think if you allow yourself to look deeply, what you'll discover is that what we want is to be the container within which these experiences can be held, to be *big enough* to allow and experience them, without shrinking away. It's normal to avoid painful experiences and to wish them out of our lives, but the larger opportunity – and dare I say it, *the reality of the path* - is to embrace and allow, so that when they do show up (and they will), you can *have the experience*, rather than it having you. This is true freedom, and with true freedom comes true power to create.

> *Do not live your life to avoid dying.*
> *Die while still alive and be free to live your life.*

DYING TO BE ALIVE

Now let's look at one of our biggest fears: the fear of death. Over the years in all the reading and research I've done, I've been surprised at how many successful and influential people have become that way largely through facing their fear of death. Once they became free of their fear of death, they were free to live their life. Buckminster Fuller (famous inventor, thinker, and architect) almost committed suicide in his 30's after failing miserably as a businessman. Robert Kiyosaki (best selling author of "Rich Dad, Poor Dad") faced his fear of death as a helicopter gunship pilot in Vietnam and tells a great story of "making peace with his maker" allowing him to fly free rather then flying to avoid death. Michael Caine (world class actor) faced his fear of death in the Korean War. In his subsequent pursuit to be an actor he said "If I died doing it, I didn't' care. I only go forward. After Korea, nothing could dissuade me." He was free. There are many, many examples of people *facing their fears* with the result being freedom, freedom to *live*.

These are extreme examples of actually facing death itself, but the principles are true for *any* fear. They are only as big as *we* make them, but they *are* real for us, and they do grip us, until *we* decide otherwise. This is evolution, and is a core competency for you as a NexGen Human – facing and embracing your fears thereby creating more freedom and love in your life, *and* the lives of others.

I want to once again point out the paradox we are dealing with here. On the one hand, what you focus on expands, and on the other hand, what you resist persists.

"Resisting" and "avoiding" are actually ways of <u>focusing</u> on something.

Can you see this? To resist something you have to maintain your awareness of it on some level – you have to <u>know</u> what you are resisting – so this keeps your attention on it at some level and therefore actually brings it into your experience. So while we do not want to focus on and expand, and thereby actually create, our fears, we must release our resistance to them to become truly free of them. We do this by *embracing* and *allowing* them – note that this is very different from *focusing on* and *expanding* – we are simply embracing and allowing them into our awareness – no longer resisting them.

So this is the paradox, that to be free of your fears you must embrace and allow them.

The logical mind does not understand this. It thinks that to keep something from happening in our life we must resist, avoid, and fight against it - so that's what it does. Notice that whatever you resist, avoid,

FIGHTING THE BAD GUYS

As you may or may not know, dreams are an amazing place of transformation. A lot is going on in our dreams – our fears and fantasies play themselves out, and our subconscious and even spirit communicate to us through our dreams. This is a powerful playing ground for evolution.

At one point in my life, I was unconsciously deeply entrenched in my subconscious limiting beliefs, *trying to get rid of the bad parts of myself*, trying to transform those parts of myself I did not like and did not want in my life – and I was experiencing a fair amount of suffering. And then I had this dream that was very enlightening for me.

I was in the house I grew up in – significantly so, but not as a child – I was there as an adult. And there were several intruders, or bad guys in the house. It was nighttime and they were not supposed to be there. So being the brave man that I was, I picked up a baseball bat and started beating these guys like crazy. However, no matter how much I beat them, they bounced back and beat me back with their baseball bats. For every amazing blow I delivered to them, they each delivered one back at me equally as powerful. And after awhile of doing this I realized there was no beating these guys and they were not

leaving. So out of exasperation, I just stopped, I dropped my bat down at my side, and INTERESTINGLY, when I did that, I noticed each of them did exactly the same. They were each there, but if I didn't bother them, they didn't bother me, if I didn't pay attention to them, they didn't pay attention to me. And they even started to lose their "realness," they became more white and transparent, kind of like ghosts, the less I paid attention to them. They were in the house – my house – but were slowly losing their presence.

Now, in dreamwork, what a dream means is entirely up to you – it's your dream and you are the only person who can interpret it for you. Others may have their interpretation, but that's THEIR interpretation – and if they had your dream, that's how THEY would interpret it FOR THEM. So for me, how I interpreted this dream, was these bad guys that were in my childhood home were the parts of myself I did not want to own, they were the parts of me I had labeled bad and that I was actively rejecting and trying to change and get rid of. And me beating them with my baseball bat represented me doing this to them. Now, the insight or wisdom I got – which I believe was my higher self communicating to me through my dream – was that "the more I beat on them, or resist them, the more they will beat on me and resist me – the more presence they have in my psyche, and the more pain I will experience." This was my lesson. And in my dream when I stopped beating them up (which was really myself), and ALLOWED them to be there, they stopped beating me up and started losing their power and presence, even through they were still there. And that's an important distinction, because they didn't go away immediately, which is what I wanted, but they were no longer causing me pain, and did eventually start losing their presence.

Wow. What a gift. So that next morning, I stopped beating myself up and immediately started accepting and allowing those parts of myself that I had been up until that point rejecting and trying to get rid of. And in that moment,

and from that moment on, I experienced an incredible amount of release from the self-imposed suffering I was creating.

Now it's important to notice that my MIND could not have conceived of this – because the mind, as we will continue to discover – thinks that allowing something creates more of it, hence the only way to get rid of something is to resist it and make it wrong....which is exactly what I was doing. When I was "out of my mind" in a dream state, my higher self was able to communicate to me a higher truth through the dramatic symbolism, and very real (if you've ever experienced those very real dreams you know what I'm talking about) experience – it was very effective, and I got the lesson. I hope you can learn from my dream too and allow and embrace ALL parts of yourself. It's the only path to peace in your house.

and fight against tends to stay around in your life for you to continue resisting, avoiding, and fighting against it. This is because the mere act of resisting, avoiding, and fighting against it keeps your awareness and focus on that thing and keeps it present in your life. As a NexGen Human you know that the paradoxical path to being free of your fears is through embracing and allowing them. This will free you to focus on and create what it is you truly want in your life. It's kind of like that Chinese finger lock game, the more you try to pull your fingers out the more they become locked in. Only by *going into and embracing* the lock does the lock become free so you can then pull your fingers out. As long as you are avoiding and resisting your fears, you are not free to create.

As a NexGen Human, you are a *creator*, not an avoider. In fact, this is a great question to ask at any moment "Am I creating or avoiding?" If avoiding, identify what you are avoiding, question it's reality, and do some work to get it outside of you where you can work with it and move it through (write it down, talk it over with others, etc.). Then, when whatever you were avoiding has loosened it's grip, *choose* what you desire to *create* (rather than what you are trying to avoid). Now that is *major* transformation! And is a core skill of a NexGen Human.

The Tyranny of Fear and Threat-based Motivation

The big fears are obvious fears. What can be even more challenging to distinguish and become free of are the smaller fears, but fears nonetheless. Again, the practice is noticing in your life what is motivating you to action. Where are the thoughts and feelings coming from? Are they coming from fear, or love. After you transcend the big fears, you'll find a bunch of little ones lurking in the background. But make no mistake, they eat away at your peace and presence just as much. Here's some examples that are a bit more sneaky and maybe not as obvious at first glance:

- The <u>need</u> to achieve: Achieving anything because if you don't you won't be happy, fulfilled, successful, etc. OR because you fear what others will think if you don't
- Fear of regrets: Doing something because if you don't you might regret it later
- Feeling obligated: Attending an event (party, meeting, family gathering, social event, etc.) because if you didn't others will think

badly of you, someone will be disappointed in you, etc. – this can even include feeling obligated to answer the phone, answer the door, check email, or whatever is *running you* and you are *obligated* to attend to

+ Waking up early in the morning, because if you don't, you won't... OR because "the early bird gets the worm" (notice the scarcity thinking and fear in this belief: there aren't enough worms to go around and I won't get one if I don't get up early)
+ Going to bed early, because if you don't......

As a NexGen Human, the first thing to notice is fear-based thoughts, feelings, and actions are usually followed by some kind of "threat."

Fear-based thoughts, feelings, and actions are usually followed by some kind of *threat*. In other words, "something bad will happen if you don't do X." Whenever fear is running your life, you are not free and you are not experiencing Love. Small, everyday fears and their implicit threats combine in what's been called a GSA or a *Gnawing Sense of Anxiety*. This GSA can become the background hum to our lives, a kind of static noise that prevents us from being fully relaxed. As a NexGen Human, who knows that Love is at the core of every thing, you absolutely question the "bad things will happen" mentality. One-by-one, you begin to transcend and release these false, fear-based beliefs.

Now, I am not saying don't achieve great things, and I am not saying don't go to bed early or wake up early, or attend dinner parties, family gatherings, social events, or any of that. What I am saying is don't do these from a place of fear. Do them because you <u>choose</u> to, not because you have to. Do them to create what you truly desire in life, not to avoid what you don't want. Victims are afraid of bad things happening

71

and because of that, they take actions to avoid bad things happening. Ironically, through these actions they actually experience, at some level, those bad things mentally and emotionally, since that is the *source* of their actions. Creators are not afraid of bad things happening, they are free of bad things happening, and focus on and create what they want, because that is what they want, not because they are avoiding something else bad. NLP (Neuro Linguistics Programming) has a similar distinction with its "away from" motivation vs. "toward" motivation. "Away from" motivation is fear-based motivation driving one to avoid "bad things happening." "Toward" motivation is motivation that is more vision-based, more focused on creating what one desires, rather than avoiding what one does not want.

> *As a NexGen Human you are free and present to Love*
> *in the living and creation of your life.*

Here's an interesting side note about transcending fears. At one point in my life I was getting extreme about focusing on the positive and being the creator of my life. And I looked at my auto insurance bills and said "Isn't this an affirmation of what I don't want? An auto accident?" Why don't I focus on "safe, accident free driving" and then drop my auto insurance (I know you legally cannot, what I would do is reduce it to the lowest level). Intuitively, I knew this was not the right thing, but I persisted in looking at this. Then a conversation with a very wise woman set me straight, she said "Roger, insurance is what you pay to ensure you do not have any accidents. You set it up so there is no fear of an accident and you pay the bills every month knowing you will not have one – and that even if you did, it would not be a problem." (Remember the format: While I do not prefer <u>to have an accident,</u> I am not afraid). Now that made sense, and this thinking can be applied to many areas of life.

The Power of Shadow Work

Another term for this work of embracing your fears is *Shadow Work*. We tend to keep these fears, especially our deep rooted fears established in childhood, hidden in the dark. We tend to avoid acknowledging them and they tend to stay in the shadows. One way to look at these shadow parts of ourselves is as old commitments that we originally put in place to protect us – that we put in place to protect us when our mental, emotional, and spiritual capacities were not developed enough to be capable of withstanding some of the circumstances we were experiencing. Hence, we created automatic protection mechanisms to shield us from the pain. And they worked – they kept us alive and safe for the most part. However, now that we are older, more mature, with much, much larger perspectives on the world and what is *really* going on, these childhood protection mechanisms typically create more pain than they prevent. We've simply outgrown them and it's time to thank them and let them go. This is the essence of shadow work. Discovering, acknowledging, embracing, healing, integrating, and releasing, old commitments and old thoughts about ourselves and the world, and creating new ones.

We have a shadow, or a dark side, because the light is shining on us.

The shadow only becomes a shadow, or limiting, when you are inspired by something larger, when you are present to a greater vision of yourself and life. One of the best shadow work books I have ever read is by Debbie Ford called *The Secret of the Shadow – The Power of Owning Your Whole Story*. In this book Debbie posits that our deepest wounds are our greatest gifts *because* they impel us to compensate for them – their pain has been a source of inspiration (in a way) for us to overcome them.

At this highest level of shadow work you recognize the blessing they actually are (rather than the curse we typically consider them) and the central role they have played in making you who you are and creating the experience you are having. The shift that takes place is from resisting these beliefs, to accepting them and moving on to higher levels of creation in your life.

There is no one and no thing to transform, but yourself.

As we saw in the previous chapter, the two worlds of victim vs. creator are 100% completely and totally different worlds. It is a *huge* shift. As a NexGen Human you are able to create authentic choice by becoming bigger, and more trusting, than your small self fears. Access to the world of the creator is through evolving yourself. Evolving yourself means embracing and transcending your fears, restoring your authentic choice and making room for deeper and deeper experiences of love.

This is Evolution.
This is what it's all about.
And this is what there is to do.

What are SLB's and what might they look like?

SLB is a term I made up that stands for Subconscious Limiting Belief. These could also be called "Previous Commitments Becoming Conscious" or PCBC, because we typically made these decisions about the world and ourselves (and resulting commitments for who we are going to be about it) long ago in our lives. We then reinforced those beliefs over and over again, and kept our commitments with integrity, until they went subconscious and became *just the way the world is* (for us). Its important to note that a belief in and of itself is not limiting, it only becomes limiting when you are *inspired to grow beyond it*. So you are, at the same time, both inspired to a greater vision of yourself, and limited by old beliefs, habits, and patterns. As you might imagine this can be a frustrating place to be. And on your Hero's Path, on your path of evolution, this will be a common experience. However, over time, it's an experience that you'll eventually be able to powerfully navigate with grace and ease.

As a way of helping you distinguish what SLBs can look like, I'll share with you a couple of mine that I've been working with for some time. One of my biggest and most challenging has been "I'll screw it up and disappoint others" – or said more simply "I'm a disappointment." This stems from a variety of childhood experiences where making a mistake was not tolerated and I experienced hurt feelings as a result. Over time I reinforced this and came to *believe* this about myself – that "I'll screw it up and disappoint others" and that "I am a disappointment." As you can imagine, these experiences were not experiences I wanted to repeat, hence I created the response (and committed to it) that "since I will screw it up and disappoint others, therefore I won't even try." Now you can see just how debilitating this belief could be for an adult where engaging and learning new things happens all the time (all part of the Hero's Journey).

Over time I developed a variety of coping mechanisms, for example to carefully "assess the risk of failure." If I thought I could succeed, then I would do it. If there was a high chance of failure, however, my anxiety was high and I would avoid any action. Another favorite coping strategy was to become a super planner and analyzer, to the point of often experiencing analysis paralysis. In line with Debbie Ford's assertion that our deepest wounds create our greatest gifts, you can see that developing the ability to carefully assess risk is a good skill to have, as is a strong ability to plan and analyze. These are actually strengths I have built in response to an underlying belief that "I will screw up and disappoint others." The only problem with these strengths, was that they were *compensating mechanisms* sourced from the limiting belief. Because I believed "I will screw it up and disappoint others" I assessed risks, planned, and analyzed. The assessing, planning, and analyzing, was all done **not** for its own sake, but TO AVOID screwing it up and disappointing others. This underlying belief was *running me* – and it manifested for me in my life many times. It showed up as failure. No amount of assessing, planning, and analyzing was going to overcome the very powerfully held belief that "I will screw it up and disappoint others." That was ultimately the strongest belief and that was what I would manifest, even though it was largely subconscious!

Once I discovered and became <u>conscious</u> of this belief I had about myself, THE EVOLUTIONARY OPPORTUNITY TO EMBRACE AND RELEASE IT BECAME AVAILABLE.

In transforming this belief I experienced an incredible amount of new found freedom. As an example, this book would not have been written had I not done this inner world work. I also experienced a huge increase in love, mostly self-love (that I am not a disappointment), and that is priceless.

Now, interestingly, even though I had this subconscious belief about myself, I succeeded at many things in life (most people probably had no idea I had this SLB running my life). Ironically, where I tended to succeed was in areas and with things that didn't really matter to me. For example I found getting college degrees and working in full time corporate roles relatively easy to succeed at – I didn't particularly *enjoy* it, but it didn't *really matter* to me, hence my perceived risk of failure was low – "if I fail, so what, it doesn't really matter to me anyhow." I was free to succeed because I wasn't *afraid* to fail.

On the flip side of this, and where I tended to "fail" or simply avoid, was in those areas that <u>really</u> mattered to me. These were areas of my life where I was very vulnerable and could really get hurt if I failed. So, when it came to being a leader in the field of personal growth and transformation, I found myself scared to death! Why? Because it really mattered to me. It was a direct threat to my subconsciously held belief, my perceived risk of failure and hurt was high, and hence so were my anxiety levels. I was so afraid to fail that I was not free to succeed. Unbeknownst to me, my subconscious fears were running the show. (We'll explore more about the divine nature of this setup in Chapter VII "The Power of Your Purpose," and how your most important mission on this planet, your purpose, will be your most transformational path).

Another area in which this belief was confronted was in intimate relationships. Note that I didn't say "I" confronted this belief – "I," my conscious self, did not confront this belief. IT was automatically activated without my conscious knowing! IT was running ME subconsciously. My conscious mind wanted one thing, but my subconscious mind was already, and more powerfully, committed to something else. So in the area of intimate relationships, I could easily date women who were not a threat to me, but when it came to a woman I might truly Love (and who could really reject and hurt me), my belief and fear of "I'll screw it up and disappoint" was running my behaviors like crazy - although again, subconsciously, so I didn't even know it – I just knew I was comfortable and free with some women (although not inspired and fulfilled), and was scared of other women and unable to be with them. What was really going on was my SLB was being activated, my anxiety went up, and I therefore avoided the situation.

Consciousness itself is healing.

- DR. WILL JOEL FRIEDMAN

It's very important to note that for most of my life these beliefs were completely subconscious. It's like water to a fish – undistinguished – you just can't see it, but it's running your life! However, when you are waking up to these mechanisms in your life, *and you are stepping onto your true path of fulfillment,* you'll get serious about distinguishing what's running you – and you'll begin the process of making conscious what has up until now been unconscious. Why? Because you are up to bigger and greater things! The vision of your life demands it! Your *desire* to be free to CONSCIOUSLY CREATE your life becomes far greater than the "safety and comfort" these old SLBs have been providing (what used to be safety is now imprisonment). You come to a point where it's time to evolve yourself and fulfill your mission. The time has come to evolve beyond the childhood fears and beliefs that have been running your life.

As a NexGen Human you celebrate the amazing transformational opportunity that your SLB's present to you. You embrace and allow them, see them for what they are (SLBs created long ago) and evolve into the conscious creator you are destined to be.

PROCESSING, JUST ENOUGH

I want to talk a little bit about processing one's problems, which is partially what this chapter – It's All About Evolution - is about. It's important to avoid getting stuck in and wallowing in our problems. In life there is a just right balance that we want to support – plants need water, but not too much water, plants need sun, but not too much sun – and we need to face our fears and work through our unique challenges and problems, but not get stuck there in that processing mode.

There is a time in life where processing is necessary and going there is the courageous and right thing to do. But eventually you come to a point where there are significantly diminishing returns in the ongoing engagement of an issue or area. It's possible that the ongoing engagement of an issue or challenge will only give it energy and keep it alive and present in your life. As a NexGen Human I want you to be aware of this going in and be looking for that place where you intuitively know it's time to move on.

How fast you get to this place mostly depends on your desire to be healed and the vision you have for your life. Especially the power of the vision you have for your life, I think that is KEY. Without a vision there is nothing calling you forward (that's why one of the chapters in this book is The Power of Your Purpose). Until you define your purpose, your divinely inspired mission, you are running from your pain with no inspiration for creation. Notice that it's easier to wallow around in endless processing of problem after problem if you do not have a compelling vision that inspires you to heal yourself and move on.

I am inspired to be a force of healing and transformation for others - to lead groups, write books, connect people to their hearts and live the lives they are meant to be living. I also have a vision of my life as financially free, abundant, fun, and loving - virtually none of that is possible with me as a victim, with me continuing to carry my wounds - and be right - comfortably uncomfortable, in my miserable, yet predictable pattern and state. How do I know none of that is possible? Because that is exactly what happened to me. I had a track record of taking myself out, time and time again, so my vision was never manifesting. After trying and trying, I eventually got smart and got a therapist – who is really just a professionally trained, powerful partner for inner world exploration - and I started looking into my shadows and what was going on in my subconscious.

This is when my most dramatic healing started taking place.

My point is shadow work is important, is essential and there is far too much disrespect for it. Maybe people did too much "navel gazing" in the 60s and 70s, and like everything the pendulum swung too far. But it's time now to restore the sacred path of the Hero's Journey and to support people in engaging the appropriate amount of their own, internal work of personal healing, transformation and evolution.

I think too many leaders today do not appreciate the profound work most people need to do to unwind and understand the subconscious patterns that are running their life. I'm not saying everyone has to do this, but I'm saying many people probably do. Take a good honest look for yourself and be willing to go there, for yourself AND for others. Where are you pretending everything is OK? Where do you feel hurt or afraid? This is a deep and profound work, a noble work, for you to take on. It is not selfish and it is not self indulgent. People who see it this way probably still have their own issues to work out and are afraid to go there. Yes it can be scary and difficult work - it is nothing less than a full paradigm shift of your world - it is liberation of your spirit. It is the HERO'S journey. It is what everyone talks about, but very few honestly do.

One way to tell how complete, free, and liberated a person is (including yourself) is by the duration of silence they can stand, especially in the presence of chaos. You can also tell how liberated and free a person is, how whole and complete they are, by how much control they need to have in their life. If they need and demand a lot, trying to get everyone around them to do their things, or rushing around trying to get themselves to do all the things they think they need to do, they likely have lots of internal work left to do. If however, they are relatively free and trusting, inspiring action in others and trusting the Universe and trusting the process, then they have come quite far. This is the aspiration of a NexGen Human.

Questions for Reflection

+ What do you suspect are some of your Subconscious Limiting Beliefs? How do they run you?

+ In what areas of your life can you see you are more run by fear than love? Are you willing to embrace and allow those fears and begin choosing to create from a place more based in love?

+ How much time do you spend thinking about the past? How much time do you spend worrying about the future? Write down a ratio. What's left is the amount of time you spend in the present. Given that the present moment is all there is, *where are you* most of the time? If most of your time is spent in the past or future, where you are is *in your mind*, out of the present moment with life literally passing you by while you are in your head *thinking about* the past or worrying about the future. Is there an opportunity for you to become more aware and in the present moments of your life?

+ How much of your time is filled with wonder, awe, joy, and love? Notice these things exist mostly in the present moment as *experiences*. Can you see that *thinking about joy* is far different from actually *experiencing* it?

OPPORTUNITIES FOR ACTION

+ Set aside 10 minutes to sit down and make a list of all your fears – an exhaustive list – put them all out there and on there (note: the first fear you may have to embrace is your fear of embracing your fears! If so, make that number one on your list, then get on with the exercise). This alone will be transformational. Now take one, whichever one feels intuitively appropriate to you at this time, one that if you loosened its grip you'd definitely experience more freedom, and embrace it. Ask that fear what it has to teach you. Ask that fear what it is protecting you from. Thank that fear for protecting you. Now, ask that fear what it needs from you so it can relax, so it can let go, and you can live your life more freely. Give it what it needs.

+ Now, imagine as if it has already happened. Now what? Look to really see "If this really happened to me, then where would I be and what would I do?" What do you notice?

+ What are the things in your life that irritate, frustrate, anger, displease, or simply bother you?" List these out. These are things you can transcend and let go of – the more you let go of these things, the more peace and joy you will experience. Ask yourself "what do I want?" more joy, happiness and peace? Or to continue resisting these things in my life trying to change them and thereby guaranteeing myself more frustration, anger, etc.?

POWERFUL RESOURCES

+ Beyond Belief Audio Program: Shift It – Accessing the Gift Within. This is a powerful tool designed to transform blocks, challenges, and issues into opportunities. It uses the energy and intelligence of your higher self to reveal the gift within each problem, challenge, or block. It is designed with busy lives in mind and can be completed in less than 20 minutes. www.GoBeyondBelief.com/products.php

+ Book: *The Secret of the Shadow: The Power of Owning Your Whole Story* by Debbie Ford

+ Book: *Transitions: Making Sense of Life's Changes – Strategies for Coping with the Difficult, Painful, and Confusing Times in Your Life* by William Bridges – this book does an amazing job of distinguishing the terrain of our life's transitions. It is essential reading to understand what is happening when we experience the inevitable changes that we all go through in life, from big to small. My favorite quote in this book refers to the Peanuts character Linus and how during our life's transitions we can feel like Linus when his blanket is in the dryer. This book will help you make sense of your life's transitions, let go of the rock you are clinging to, and swim to the other side.

+ Book: *The Welcoming Process* by Frank M. Lobsiger – this book presents an amazing new process for transforming and evolving yourself. Frank, a good friend of mine, realized that the biggest source of suffering in human life was SELF criticism, judgment, and rejection. In other words <u>we are our own worst enemies</u>. And that therefore one of the keys to the peace, freedom, love, and joy that is universally desired by humans, is our ability to cultivate Self Love – or, ones ability to love oneself. Based on years of research, personal experience, and application in practice, Frank has developed a cutting edge tool and process – "The Welcoming Process" – that is simple, really works, and enables us to embrace today's unique evolutionary opportunities (at the time of this writing, the book was not yet available, but imminent).

+ Book: *The Enneagram – Understanding Yourself and the Others in Your Life* by Helen Palmer – From the Introduction "The Enneagram is an ancient Sufi teaching that describes nine different personality types and their interrelationships. The teaching can help us to recognize our own type and how to cope with our issues; understand our work associates, lovers, family, and friends; and to appreciate the predisposition that each type has for higher human capacities such as empathy, omniscience, and love." I recommend this book because it can do exactly what this introductory paragraph says. It has helped me better understand my *personality pre-dispositions* and how these are transformed over time through my higher self. It has also helped me better understand and appreciate the life pathways of others. Keep in mind this is just another model and is not the truth or absolutely how things are. If you are attracted to it, you can use it as a tool to reflect back to yourself your own truths and beliefs about the world and thereby better orient yourself within it. One of the interesting things to note is that each of the 9 personality types is basically dealing with their own unique Subconscious Limiting Beliefs, and that the journey into their evolved selves is essentially the journey of discovering and evolving beyond their unique SLBs. I am a Nine on the Enneagram, which is known as "The Mediator," and it makes perfect sense that I would be writing this book and doing the work I am doing as I work through my unique SLBs, deepen my connection to Source, and embrace my authentic life path and mission. Get the book and check it out for yourself. It can provide some powerful insights and another perspective, or map, for your evolution.

- *Various Models for the Evolution of Consciousness* – there are many models for the evolution of consciousness. These models can be helpful as maps and guides to the terrain, and can help you understand where you are, where you've been, where you're going, and some of the challenges and opportunities you are likely to encounter along the way. Three models that I have found very helpful in this sense are:

o "The Energetic Dimensions of Manifestation" found on page 23 of the book *The Intelligent Heart* by David McArthur and Bruce McArthur. This chart divides the evolution of consciousness into three major stages, with the middle stage having several levels. The model is relatively simple and because of that it is very powerful. One thing the authors point out is that the evolution of consciousness is not a linear process – we can experience different levels in different areas of our lives at different times as we progress to higher and wider stages.

o "Map of the Scale of Consciousness" appendix B, page 424 of the book *Reality and Subjectivity* by David R. Hawkins, M.D., Ph. D. David Hawkins uses kinesiology, or muscle testing, as a measurement of "awareness of truth" or level of consciousness. He has 17 different levels, ranging from Shame to Enlightenment, that calibrate along a scale from 0 to 1000. Besides illuminating that there are multiple levels of awareness one can evolve to and through, another powerful insight from this scale is that until a human being passes through the first 8 levels and begins to establish integrity in and with their life, they are weak in their ability to consciously create by choice.

o *Spiral Dynamics* is a system which was first proposed by Clare Graves. Many people have found this model helpful in understanding the various stages of consciousness we tend to evolve through as human beings. Again, a map like this should not be looked at as *the truth*, but rather as helpful guidance and insight as we navigate our own evolutionary path.

Chapter VI

ONE STEP AT A TIME

*One of the greatest myths of our time
is that transformation happens in an instant.*

Have you noticed that life has a certain inertia to it, and when you press in on it, it tends to press back a bit? It's called homeostasis. In their book, *The Life We Are Given* (Tarcher Putnam, 1995) George Leonard and Michael Murphy point out "Our body, brain, and behavior have a built-in tendency to stay the same within rather narrow limits and to snap back when changed – and it's a very good thing they do." It's what keeps your body together and all its systems running smoothly. The body works very hard at maintaining homeostasis and keeping things normal. Homeostasis is the natural resistance or tendency of the Universe to maintain the status quo.

This does NOT mean things don't change; things are always changing. They change over time, however, ONE STEP AT A TIME. And as you travel your path of growth and transformation you are definitely going to run into this naturally occurring phenomenon. Knowing about it in advance will help you identify the mechanism when it shows up and wisely continue on your path. Transformation *can* happen in an instant, but it usually doesn't.

Expecting a Miracle

One of my greatest disappointments, and lessons, was my expectation that I could take a weekend or week long workshop and totally transform myself. This does not in any way decrease the value I received from the many workshops and programs I attended. Every single one them contributed to my life, but the false promises and expectations of "amazing transformations" from a weekend workshop are mostly hopeful hype. Maybe 10% of the people who attend a workshop actually DO create an amazing breakthrough and experience profound change immediately after the program. So it's not that it's not possible. But what I will suggest is that these people **were already well along** their transformational path, had been working on their area or issue(s) of interest for quite some time, and were NOW ready for a breakthrough. While the program may have been the catalyst or provided that final clarifying insight, the work that person had been doing *prior* to that program laid the essential groundwork for the breakthrough.

> *As a NexGen Human you know that breakthroughs*
> *CAN happen in a moment,*
> *BUT are usually created over time.*

Now let's stop right here and notice something. Notice that your *mind wants and expects* a miracle. This is often what we are hoping for as we purchase some program, product, or process. This is what we are being "sold." Isn't it tantalizing to fantasize about some miracle that is going to happen to us that will instantly change our lives for the better, forever? It is, isn't it. However, this is also how your mind (small self, ego self) maintains control and keeps everything at status quo. By expecting a miracle and never getting it, your mind is able to undermine the true process of change. It says "Well THAT didn't work, and THAT didn't work, and THAT didn't work." This attitude slows you down by distracting you from any growth you ARE achieving and discouraging you from engaging any more. Once you stop *expecting* the miracle instant cure, you can actually get on with the *real* process of personal growth and make real changes.

NATURAL TRANSFORMATION OVER TIME

The tomato plant goes from seed to gorgeous tomato OVER TIME. A baby is created and becomes a baby over 9 months. The tomato plant and baby are good examples because so much happens behind the scenes where you can't see it – under the earth and in the womb. It would be easy to assume nothing is happening since you can't see it. However, you would be very mistaken (setting ultrasound and the enlarging mother's belly aside, there is still a lot going on that is out of sight). Then BOOM!, in a relatively short instant the tomato plant breaks through the surface of the earth, and BOOM! the baby is born, and both the baby and the tomato plant begin to very obviously grow and our minds are relieved because we can now see the progress and trust that all is OK. But it is *still* happening one step at a time. The baby grows into a man or woman over years! And the tomato takes months before it is ready to eat. These are natural processes of living organisms growing and transforming in the world, just like we are, and it doesn't happen in a weekend.

> *Much of what we are exposed to completely dishonors the natural process of transformation, growth, and learning.*

We all want our happiness, success, and wealth in an instant and we are all too ready to believe the promises of someone saying they can give it to us. Many "Fast-Track to Success" seminars do a major disservice to those new on the path by setting them up for disappointment.

Let's take the baby example. Here's the seminar pitch you hear on the radio: "Tired of waiting for babies to be born? Want the beauty and brilliance of a baby of your own without having to wait? Come to the "Your Baby Now" Seminar where you will learn how to create a real human baby in only 2 days! Yes, that's right, from conception to delivery in just 2 days! This amazing miracle has been transforming the lives of thousands. Call now!" Of course this is ridiculous, but the example points to the absurdity of ignoring natural law. Your growth and expansion are no different.

Promises for amazing transformation are rampant, especially in key areas of life such as health, wealth, and relationships. The truth is YOU CAN transform yourself and any area of your life, and programs and products CAN and DO help you do this. At the right moment, the right program can bring on a catharsis, a breakthrough, or a significant insight. All of these contribute to your growth. However, the REALIZATION of most breakthroughs, as recognizable change on a day-to-day basis, happens over time not over night. If change does manifest instantaneously after a breakthrough, you've likely been working on that area or issue prior to the workshop/seminar. If you haven't been working on that breakthrough prior to the workshop, then it's likely you'll be working on its manifestation and realization into your life AFTER the breakthrough, over time. Either way, it didn't miraculously fully manifest into your life in an instant. Like the old saying goes: "It takes a lifetime to create an overnight success." Ask any successful person in any arena. If you can get their *true* story rather than the nutshell or magical version, you'll discover it took them years. And even if they did produce some amazing result in what appears to be a year or two, if you look closely, you'll find that in the years before the crucial 1 or 2, they were working toward that "magical" success in one way or another. The truth is, in ALL areas, it's a process. It takes time! What we are talking about here is your personal process of evolution and growth as a human being.

As a NexGen Human you are wise,
you respect the natural process of life,
and you take it one step at a time.

SHOUTING AT THE SEQUOIA

Another version of this belief, that you can transform yourself in an instant, involves what I call "Shouting at the Sequoia." Sequoia redwoods are the tallest trees in the world; they can grow as high as 350 feet with a base that is 20 feet in diameter. Imagine a Sequoia that is 5 or 6 years old; it has come a long way from the seed it started out as and is doing quite well. It has grown to 10 feet tall, has a trunk that is a few inches in diameter, and roots that reach several feet into the ground. It has branches full of long, flat leaves that reach in all directions, soaking up the sun. The tree is quite happy in nature unfolding as it has been for the past few years. Then a bird comes along, lands on a branch of this tree and says to the young Sequoia "You know, you could be a lot more than you are right now. There are trees right here in this grove that are 150 feet tall with roots that go deep into the earth with trunks many feet in diameter. They are most grand and live a very blessed and happy life indeed. If you were more like them you would be happier, more respected, more successful, and you would have everything you want." The young Sequoia hears all this and starts to feel something it's never felt before, a discomfort of some kind, a dis-content. It starts to feel inadequate, suddenly who and what it is, is no longer sufficient somehow. It wants to be 150 feet tall, with roots deep in the earth, its trunk many feet in diameter. It wants to be grander, and happier, more respected, and more successful. For the first time in its life, the little Sequoia has actually become unhappy. So it starts on a quest to become more like the big trees, for it knows that will make it more happy. Everything it does is focused on trying to make its roots deeper, its trunk bigger, and its branches reach higher. It is shouting at itself: "Come on, hurry up, bigger, deeper, higher." The tree expends a huge amount of energy and experiences much suffering and struggle. And actually, over time, there is some progress. Over the years its roots do go deeper, its trunk does get wider, and its branches do reach higher – but it's never enough, and it's never fast enough. So the Sequoia continues to be unhappy wishing it was more, bigger, better, and of course happier.

> *What the Sequoia has forgotten, is that just like you,*
> *it is supported by a natural process,*
> *that over time will have ALL these things happen,*
> *exactly the way they should for its perfect growth path*
> *without all the suffering, unhappiness, and struggle.*

I'm sure you can see just how ridiculous this is for a Sequoia tree, but can you see it for yourself? As a human being, can you hear who's shouting? We are all perfectly unfolding and naturally inspired to take some actions and not others. The Sequoia, *in its natural process of growth,* may hit a rock with one of its roots. It was going along in one direction, then boom, it hits a rock and has to grow in another direction. This is perfectly normal and natural. Rocks exist in the earth, and roots know to grow around them and continue to expand. The rain comes down, the sun shines upon it, and the soil provides the nutrients. THE TREE DOES NOT HAVE TO DO A THING for these elements to come to it. In fact, if the elements were not there in the first place, the tree would not exist at all! All the Sequoia has to do is trust it's unfolding, all of it—rocks, bird sh*t, wood peckers, squirrels, cloudy days, hot days, no rain, too much rain—and UNFOLD, without struggle, without suffering, without fear, and without CONTROL! Just be the Sequoia it is at each stage of its life, happy in each and every moment knowing it's LIFE IS UNFOLDING IN THE PERFECT TIME FOR THE HIGHEST GOOD OF ALL. Because it is! If you can see that for the Sequoia, you can see that for your own life.

As millionaire, author, and founder of New World Library Marc Allen has said in his book *The Type-Z Guide to Success – A Lazy Person's Manifesto for Wealth and Fulfillment* affirm now and affirm often: MY LIFE IS PERFECTLY UNFOLDING, IN A RELAXED AND EASY WAY, IN ITS OWN PERFECT TIME, FOR THE HIGHEST GOOD OF ALL.

Doesn't that feel great? You can trust the natural unfolding of your life – without all the screaming, yelling, struggling, worrying, and forcing. Where the heck are you "getting to" anyways?

You have everything you need to become the greatest most fantastic you. You wouldn't be here if you didn't. And it IS happening – you are right now unfolding and growing, each and every day into greater and greater expressions of yourSelf.

What there is for you to do is TRUST THAT, and ALLOW that – ONE STEP AT A TIME. As a NexGen Human you find true joy and happiness in partnering with this Universal Life Force and consciously experiencing its movement through you. Allowing it's movement through you and unfolding, one step at a time, your magical amazing self. Once you understand, appreciate and allow this POWERFUL natural process to *unfold you* you will realize in each and every moment YOU ARE <u>ALWAYS</u> EVERYTHING YOU CAN BE. And here's a little secret: anyone who says to you otherwise, and is critical, judgmental, and forceful regarding how *they* think you *should* be, has their own expectations and B.S. going on. Don't let them crap in your world! And get out of theirs if you have to. These are people with low self esteem that are not willing to own up to their own B.S. and do the work to become integrated. People who know what they are doing, and have faced their own fears of inadequacy, will *inspire* you to greater capacities, not dominate you with criticism, judgment, threats, and fear-based tactics. That is simply a projection of their world–and all their fears–out into yours. Just say no.

Crazy Making

One of the most crazy making statements we often say and hear in our society is: "You should know better." This is absolutely ridiculous because if you did, or if you really should, THEN YOU WOULD! Which makes this statement "You should know better" useless. Another crazy making and stress producing question often asked audiences in the self-development arena is: "How many of you know you could be doing better than you are?" Or, said another way: "How many of you know you could be doing more with your life than you are right now?" These statements are absolutely crazy making because they deny the reality of your life exactly as it has been, and is right now, and creates a fantasy world in which "it <u>could</u> have been different." Dr. David Hawkins, author of *Power vs. Force* calls this a "hypothetical mentation." Said simply: it's a fantasy reality in the mind that actually doesn't exist. This is a negative JUDGMENT! And as a negative judgment it holds negative energy. Sure it "could" have been different, but the fact is IT WASN'T! And the <u>truth</u> is IT IS EXACTLY THE WAY IT WAS AND IS! If you really COULD have done better, YOU WOULD HAVE DONE BETTER! Isn't that true? Check out your life RIGHT NOW. This is critical to grasp. If the "could have" proposition were true, you might as well be saying to yourself: "Well, I could do so much better than I am right now, but I'm not going to because I prefer to do worse."

In each and every moment you are ALWAYS doing the best that you can – given who you are, your skills, desires, habits, knowledge, beliefs, circumstances, etc., etc., etc. in each and every moment (and so is everyone else).

It's a debilitating fantasy to think that in your <u>past</u> you could've done better than you did – it's an ego-based, stress producing judgment of yourself that just is not true. The quicker you get related to REALITY, and stop judging your <u>past</u>, the more access you have to powerful actions in the <u>present</u>. So, from now on, as a NexGen Human, your answer to these questions, should they arise in your experience is "NO. No matter how it looks, I am ALWAYS doing the very best I can and my life is always, including right now, perfectly unfolding."

Now, this doesn't mean you can't do things differently in THIS present moment and as you <u>go forward</u>! As a NexGen Human you are always learning and always willing to try new things on your path of growth. But these new actions are taken in the present! That's the only place they can be taken. The better question is "Based on my experience from the past, is there something I can learn to help me perform better right now, in this *present moment?*" The answer is absolutely YES! This is evolution, this is growth, this is expansion. The Sequoia grows its roots and branches in many ways and many directions, building on the past, <u>exactly as it was</u>, **one step at a time.**

A Theory of Change

I have a theory that may provide some context and compassion as you consciously evolve as a NexGen Human and create your desired reality. It's a four stage theory that builds on itself to its conclusion: 1) You have probably heard the statement that every 5 to 7 years every cell in your body is new and replaced (Deepak Chopra, MD has said this, as has Quantum Physicist John Hagelin). You have an entirely new body every 5 to 7 years. Isn't that amazing?! Just that fact alone suggests you are not your body. "YOU" get a new one every 5 to 7 years, but what is the "you" that is getting it? What is the "you" that is staying around and is consistent through all that physical world change? Great and powerful questions, but not why I brought this up. 2) Quantum Biologist Bruce Lipton, author of *The Biology of Belief*, has scientifically demonstrated that our beliefs live in each and every one of our cells. Beliefs are not just "in our head" but actually are resonating in each and every cell of our entire body. This has far reaching implications for health and well being, but again, is not why I bring this up. 3) Quantum Physics, as represented in popular movies such as *What the Bleep Do We Know* and *The Secret*, posits that our thoughts and feelings create and attract our reality. If your thoughts and feelings (aka your beliefs) are creating your reality,

AND they live in your each and every cell, AND it takes 5 to 7 years to replace every cell in your body, then it stands to reason that it will take about 5 to 7 years to totally transform your beliefs and hence your life. And, 4) if you ask around and pay attention to success stories like I have, you'll find that from the time a now successful person started engaging their new field of endeavor (whatever it is), it took about 5 years until they were really experiencing the success they imagined. Over that time they transformed their beliefs, cell by cell, thought by thought, feeling by feeling, experience by experience, until most of the cells in their body were resonating the new beliefs and desires. And viola! via the laws of Quantum Physics, they were able to attract, create, and experience that reality in physical, tangible form.

Heck, the creation of this book from initial thoughts to this full manifestation has been about 5 years!

Now, a part of me resists this theory, because I want to believe I can create my reality far faster, i.e. I don't want to limit myself by *believing* it will take this long. However, what I'm talking about here is <u>life level</u> transformation and manifestation. And when it comes to manifesting on this level, where ALL our historical beliefs, patterns, and habits are challenged, I'm wise enough to stop trying to make babies in 2 days and Shouting at Sequoias to make them grow. It's just a theory, but it's proving out in my experience. Check it out for yourself, it may save you tons of frustration and disappointment, and keep you on your path.

THE FOUR STAGE MODEL –
TRANSFORMING SUBCONSCIOUS LIMITING
BELIEFS

Here's a simple model that will help you understand how the transformation and evolution of your subconscious limiting beliefs might go. This is also a map or model of how the development or learning of any new skill or competency tends to go.

Keep in mind this is just a map and is not "the truth" or necessarily how things will really go. Just like the menu at a restaurant is not the food, this map is not the actual terrain of transformation you will be traversing. However, it can provide some guidance and direction, and to the extent it helps you navigate through your transformation and better understand the process you are engaging, then it is valuable.

This is a four quadrant model that I've heard called *Abraham Maslow's Mastery Matrix*, as well as *The Learning Ladder*. I've included the model here for your reference:

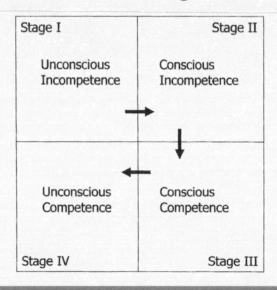

Model for Learning & Change

Stage I	Stage II
Unconscious Incompetence	Conscious Incompetence
Unconscious Competence	Conscious Competence
Stage IV	Stage III

The top left quadrant, Stage I, is where we start developing any new skill, or competency: Unconscious Incompetence. In this stage of evolution we don't know what we don't know. And in the case of our subconscious limiting beliefs, they are running our lives without our conscious awareness of it. We perceive and interact with the world the way we see it and "that's just the way it is."

Now, as a NexGen Human, as you step out onto your mission and begin engaging your personal vision, you will move into Stage II: Conscious Incompetence. You are now becoming aware of what you previously did not know. You are now aware of your incompetence in a particular arena and, in the case of a subconscious limiting belief, you are becoming aware of how they are running your life in ways that you no longer desire. Although this stage can be a bit painful, it is a MAJOR first step, because things you want to change or develop have moved from unconsciousness into your CONSCIOUS AWARENESS where you can now begin to work with them.

Over time, as you become more and more aware of how your subconscious limiting beliefs have been running your life, where they get activated, and you build your ability to *choose differently*, you move into Stage III: Conscious Competence. This is a great place to be because you are now competent at choosing and creating your life, using your new skills, empowering truly authentic choices (rather than unconsciously reacting), and therefore experiencing success in the way you now desire.

It's important to note that the majority of work in transforming your subconscious limiting beliefs will happen between Stages II and III. You will take one step forward, then two steps back, and two steps forward, then one step back. You bounce back and forth between Stages II and III, between your incompetence and your competence, until you finally develop stability: the SLB has significantly lost its grip on you and you are competently creating your life in a new, consciously empowered way. Basically you have weakened the old subconscious limiting belief and replaced it with a new, more empowering belief.

In the final stage of transformation, you move into Stage IV: Unconscious Incompetence. You become so competent at "believing" the new belief and/or using the new skill, that the new belief, skill, or competency, eventually becomes "just the way things are." At this point it moves into your unconscious mind. This is a great stage to be in because now your experience of yourself and your world, as you have consciously chosen and created it, goes basically on auto pilot. Whether it is health, wealth, love, or peacefulness, these new beliefs and skills become a deeply integral part of who you are.

Simple examples of this process that are very common are learning to tie our shoes, brush our teeth, or learning to drive. All of these things at one point in our lives were difficult for us to do. But now we do them automatically without giving it a thought. They are literally programmed into our subconscious and our ability to do these things is "just the way it is." This is also true of other "ways of being" and beliefs you have learned and practiced over the years, whether they are empowering ways for you to be or not so empowering ways.

As you step onto your Hero's Journey and really go for it in terms of manifesting your unique passions, purpose, and mission, you will experience those places in yourself ready for transformation and evolution. Keep this model in mind and you will be better able to stay on the path.

SUCCESS IS A SERIES OF FAILURES

Success is series of failures,
but nobody wants to believe this,
experience this, or talk about this.

We seem to think that if we ignore this "fact of life" it will somehow go away, or "it just won't happen to me." I listen very carefully to successful people as they talk about their path to success and I haven't heard a single person say they had no challenges or failures. However, almost all of them barely mention these experiences in their lives and very quickly gloss over their "challenges, frustrations, and failures" on their path and go right to the "good part" of success they are now experiencing. Why do they do this? Because no one wants to focus on and hear about the failures – people just want to hear about the success. No one wants to hear that they themselves may have to "fail" before they experience success. Do you? I don't. But I'd rather hear the truth than be spoon fed some fantasy. Because of the unpopularity of "challenge, frustration, and failure," these critical success elements get minimized and underappreciated as the MAJOR, CRITICAL and KEY stepping stones to success they actually are!

Due to our schooling and years of indoctrination we have an incredibly low tolerance for mistakes. As school children we learned that mistakes are bad and that getting a 100% on the test is good. If a context wherein mistakes are viewed as opportunities for learning is missing, they are represented as failures. Our education system taught us to memorize and then regurgitate facts onto a test. Perhaps as a measurement of our ability to memorize, this would not be so bad. But in the ever-changing real world, where memorized facts rarely produce the result you are looking for, this type of learning is not very effective. The REAL process of accomplishing anything will involve trial and <u>error,</u> with mistakes along the path being very common.

The classic example of this is inventor Thomas Edison. Depending on which source you look at, it took him somewhere around 1,000 attempts to finally invent the light bulb (which remains relatively unchanged to this day!). When asked by a reporter why he failed so many times, he replied (and I'm paraphrasing here) "I never failed, each trial taught me how not to make it and brought me one step closer to success." Brilliant!

I discovered another great example of this in the bonus materials on the DVD of the Academy Award winning movie *A Beautiful Mind.* In the segment on "The Making of the Movie A Beautiful Mind" the writer discusses how he literally re-wrote a scene 75 times! Each re-write had fewer and fewer words, until he finally nailed it. The scene, only seconds in duration, moves me to tears each time I watch it, but you would never know the extraordinary amount of trial and error that went on behind its creation.

Now look at these two examples. Notice these are both successful people; one as an inventor the other as a writer. They know what they are doing! They are <u>experienced</u> in the fields they are working in, and their path to success was laden with "failed" attempts. Consider that when creating or engaging something new, THIS is the mark of a true professional. He or she "learns from each attempt" (what is and is not working) and subsequently makes adjustments and <u>tries again</u>. In this context you are not experiencing failure, rather you are experiencing a *learning process*.

One of my favorite trainers is T. Harv Eker (founder of Peak Potentials Training and best selling author of *Secrets of the Millionaire Mind*). He says he failed at something like 17 different businesses before he found his niche and became a millionaire. He is known for saying "Every master was once a disaster." This very clearly points out the learning process that all, eventually masterful, people go through. He also says things like "He who makes the most mistakes fastest wins," "Fail forward fast," and "Correct and continue." All of these statements point toward the inevitable process of learning we will all experience as we engage our life path and passions.

Now, I can write about this with some authority because I have had ample opportunity to "Correct and continue" and to "engage my learning processes." I've experienced numerous "failures" along my life path and to be honest, *at the time*, they did feel like failures. It really comes down to understanding and perspective, and these we only gain over time. Today,

I can see how all of these experiences have contributed to my life path and have created who I am. Here is list of some of my "failures" and past learning opportunities: internet dot com start-up, network marketing, real estate investments, stock market investments, transformational business leadership, small business purchases, small business creation, author (yes, I engaged the writing path several times), life-coach, and relationships & engagement, to name a few. The truth is I had an expectation that was not met with each endeavor, and hence defined my experience as a "failure." As a human being, yes, it hurt. But what you won't hear from me is "victim." I take 100% responsibility and do not blame anyone or anything. I have learned incredibly valuable lessons that are becoming even more valuable as I go on – that is the process! That is the practice. That is the path. **One step at a time.**

Questions for Reflection

♦ Where are you "Shouting at the Sequoia" in your life? Where can you trust your natural unfolding more and relax into your life?

♦ What good thoughts and feelings do you have each day that you'd like to continue cultivating, experiencing, and perhaps expanding?

♦ Are there any new thoughts you might want to start cultivating, working with, and having on a regular basis?

Opportunities for Action

♦ List out all your "failures" – every single one of them, make a big, long list of your disappointments in life (just listing these out will create freedom and movement in your life). Now celebrate them! Think of all the learning these experiences have created for you. Know that, because of these experiences, you are better prepared and ready for success than ever before! Now burn that list and release any negative judgments you may still be holding regarding those experiences and allow them to be the stepping stones on your evolutionary path of success that they actually are.

POWERFUL RESOURCES

- Beyond Belief Audio Program – "Deep Relaxation & Power Visioning Process" – This program provides a unique structure inside of which you create your life's desires in the inner world of your thoughts and feelings. It is designed to be used on a regular basis to integrate, over time, your desired new beliefs into your very being. www.GoBeyondBelief.com/products.php
- Book – "The Biology of Belief – Unleashing the power of consciousness, matter, & miracles" by Bruce Lipton, Ph.D. Bruce is an inspiring and entertaining leader in the field of biology and through this book he demonstrates how our thoughts literally affect the function of our cells and how thoughts and beliefs themselves reside in each and every cell. Along the way he dispels the myth that we are prisoners of our DNA.
- Book – "Mind Power Into the 21st Century – Techniques to Harness the Astounding Powers of Thought" by John Kehoe. John is brilliant in his understanding and explanation of how our mind operates and how we can consciously go about working with it and cultivating it. One of the most important elements of practice I learned from working with John's material is the necessity of repetition and persistence. I am a member of "The Mind Power 90 Day Club," which means I did my mind power practice every day for 90 days straight. It's a powerful practice and I highly recommend it.

Chapter VII

YOUR PLACE IN THE UNIVERSE –
THE POWER OF YOUR PURPOSE

THE SORROW

The Sorrow of expression unfulfilled
The Sorrow of possibility
The Sorrow of what I am, unmanifest
The Sorrow of potential
The Sorrow of what could be, left undone
The Sorrow . . .
This is what I live for . . .
In the gap of this Sorrow –
Between what is, and
What IS. Ahhh . . .
To be human . . . divine distaste,
And inspiration to the invisible . . .
This is the tension, the juice,

> *The gas, the energy, that pulls me*
> *Forward, that keeps me looking,*
> *And wondering, what next?!*
> *What could be, what can be?!*
> *I'm an explorer, and therefore willing*
> *To look, letting go of what is, for the forever*
> *What could be . . . Ahhh, The Sorrow.*

A lot has been written about The Power of Your Purpose, and for good reason: there is a TON of power available once you find and embrace your life's purpose! Also your divine, authentic purpose is your most powerful path of evolution. You cannot achieve your dream without significantly evolving yourself. It is divinely designed this way. However, it's a paradox, because we tend to resist growth and change (remember homeostasis from Chapter VI?), we tend to resist our divine purpose *even though it is what we most desire in the world.*

Your dream will DEMAND your transformation.

This is good news! You will have to step out into the unknown and experience a new kind of discomfort, that of excitement and *knowing* you are a doing what you really came here to do. That kind of knowing, that kind of excitement, is priceless, and there is NO substitute.

THE POWER IN RAGS-TO-RICHES

We've all heard the Rags-to-Riches stories of rising to amazing levels of success from incredibly challenging places: bankruptcy, homelessness, drug addiction, depression, disease, and hardships of all kinds. These can be very inspiring stories. However, there is an element to these stories that is rarely appreciated: when life sucks that bad, there is an incredible amount of motivation to do just about anything to get out of it! People in these situations have nothing to lose and to *not* change could mean death (or at least significant ongoing suffering). This unusually high level of motivation causes them to do things they never would've done otherwise.

Unfortunately, a lot of these "Rags-to-Riches people" telling us their story, tell it to us in the context of "If I can come all the way from THERE (incredible challenge and suffering) to here (some level of success)....then you can certainly come to HERE from where you are (because you are not nearly as bad off as I was), and I will show you how." As logical as that sounds, it's not exactly true. The problem with this for the average person is that, unlike them when they initiated their change from the bottom of the pit, we, as much as we may *want* to change, are pretty damn comfortable where we are AND we have something to lose. Because of this, we do not have access to the same level of energy and motivation that they had from their suffering. Pain and suffering are VERY motivational. And since we actually do have something to lose, our risk is higher. These two things are rarely, if ever, recognized.

COMFORTABLY UNCOMFORTABLE

In the Rags-to-Riches transformation, the literal physical deprivation ("I didn't have a pot to piss in or a window to throw it out of") is extremely motivating. The challenge today is that we have 5 pots to piss in and 10 windows to throw them out of! My point is, finding your purpose at this time in history – when the standard of living is at an all time high for the largest number of people ever – is MORE challenging. We are not as motivated *because* we are pretty damn comfortable! It's pretty easy for us to just "plod along" in our day-to-day lives doing the same habitual things over and over again because our pain level is not dramatic enough to propel us to change. This is what I call "Dead Man Walking," you're not alive in any real sense of the word, but you're just too damn comfortable to do anything about it. That is until you aren't. And there's the rub.

There is still suffering in this day and age, but it's typically not of the material/physical deprivation kind. (Please don't get me wrong here, I know there are plenty of people in the world still suffering from material, physical lack. However, I am speaking to you, someone with the ability to read and enough money to buy this book. In this conversation, you are the most important person, so let's stay focused on your situation). The suffering being experienced in today's industrial, civilized countries is more a mental/emotional suffering.

In addition, our comfortable situation *itself* can intensify this mental/emotional suffering; because you may have everything you need to be comfortable, but you still aren't happy! That's a bit of a mind-f*ck (please excuse the word, but strong language is required) because you think you *should* be happy given all that you have, but you aren't, so what's wrong with you? On top of that, is that just like you, everyone else is putting on their happy face out in public so it *looks* like everyone is happy. This leads to depressing questions of comparison like "How come they're happy and I'm not? And "What do they have that I don't?" A bigger house, nicer car, better job, more education, more loving spouse and family, etc.??? Chances are they really aren't happy either. But you'd never know that unless you were able to dig down and see inside the reality of their life. Just like somebody would never know that YOU aren't really happy (unless they got two martinis in you and were willing to really listen to how your life ACTUALLY is).

So, I just wanted to point out that in some ways, in today's world, it IS a bit more challenging to really step out onto the Hero's Journey, because for a large majority of us we're so damn comfortably uncomfortable. It seems like there is too much to risk. But the truth is, there is far too much to risk by <u>not</u> consciously choosing and stepping onto your Hero's Path – literally YOUR LIFE is at risk. If you desire to live joyously, with deep passion, excitement, and love, rather than numbed-out living for shallowly pleasurable moments, repeat right now after me "I choose to consciously engage my Hero's Journey." Go ahead, say it out loud - "I choose to consciously engage my Hero's Journey." Thank you. Now say this:

"The suffering of not living is far greater than the suffering of truly living – I choose to truly live."

Go ahead, say it out loud "The suffering of not living is far greater than the suffering of truly living." Nicely done. It may feel a bit scary, but doesn't it feel "good-scary"? Note: when on your authentic path, challenges come, but *suffering* really is optional. Once you master many of the skills as a NexGen Human, restore your personal power of choice, and begin to walk your authentic life path, the experience of suffering, struggle, and frustration are held in a much larger context and will occur less and less.

EVERYTHING IS ON YOUR PATH – IT'S ALL A PART OF YOUR PURPOSE

Now let's talk about finding YOUR purpose. Finding one's purpose can happen in a multitude of ways. We've all heard of people who were born knowing exactly what they're here to do. Carlos Santana tells a great story of how he <u>knew</u> he was going to be a great and famous guitar player when he was in high school. For most of us, finding our *true* purpose tends to be a bit more challenging. We have so many expectations set upon us (by parents, teachers, friends, society in general, etc.), and so many options and desires, it's truly a challenge to *know* what's right.

It certainly hasn't been easy for me! Finding my unique purpose has been mostly a long and enduring process of elimination. Not this, not this, and not this. However, in each and every experience, there was always *something* I liked about it, and *something* I learned about myself, and in this manner it has <u>all</u> been a part of my purpose and mission. For example, a major theme running through my life and in all the experiences I have engaged, has been an element of being at the cutting edge of innovation and evolution – whether creating a new process, launching a new product, or now creating a NexGen Human. Discovering this, what could be called your "Theme of Power," is key. It's a process of discovering what you like. And what we like, we tend to do well at.

When everyone is "on purpose" and doing what they love and are here to do, it's like a perfectly balanced piece of music where each instrument has a role and plays its role perfectly in the overall piece.

One person's role may be quiet and unassuming, like the percussionist playing a shaker or triangle in the background. Another person's right place may involve being bold and entertaining, like the lead guitar. No one role is more important than another. They each add their own unique element to the mix, creating what the listener experiences as an amazingly beautiful piece of music.

CHOOSING WHAT TO "DO" – FINDING YOUR PROMISED LAND

Wherever you may be in your life, one of the keys to deciding what to do next is to check and see if you will enjoy the anticipated activities that will be involved or required. I am not a fan of the "sacrifice yourself now for some payoff in the future" storyline. In fact, a wise friend of mine once told me to watch out for any philosophy or plan that suggests a "promised land in the future" if you will just sacrifice yourself now in the present. This usually requires you believe and do what <u>they</u> say, and give your time, attention, and energy, to their cause so that things will turn out for you in the future. Malarky! This is more "ego talk" negating the beauty, power, and love that is <u>always</u> available and requires no sacrifice SO THAT THEN you can experience what you want.

In looking at your life path and exploring your purpose, move toward that which gives you joy NOW.

You are on the right track when some key part of the activities you will be engaged in on a daily basis bring you joy. Without this joy, your journey will absolutely be short lived, and it will be a miserable one at that! As author Dan Millman (*Way of the Peaceful Warrior*) is known for saying "There are no ordinary moments." I encourage you to honor EACH AND EVERY heartbeat and not sacrifice a single one so you can "live sometime, someday, in the future." Remember, your actions in the present tend to become the habits and experiences of your future – if you are practicing sacrifice and practicing suffering and practicing "joy will come to me someday in the future," then this is what you will have in your future; habits and experiences that create sacrifice, suffering, and "joy someday in the future." On the other hand, if you honor, engage, and express your deepest truths now, and experience JOY NOW, these are the habits and experiences you will tend to ingrain and experience even more of in your future present moments. There IS NO PROMISED LAND TO GET TO! Let me repeat that, because it is so important in terms of your awareness as a NexGen Human: THERE IS NO PROMISED LAND TO GET TO, SOMETIME, SOMEDAY, OUT THERE IN THE FUTURE. THE PROMISED LAND IS RIGHT HERE, RIGHT NOW.

When it comes to finding your purpose, it's not about "what you can get from God," it's about finding the win-win pathway where what you want is what God wants…that's where true power lies.

The Still Small Voice

The world is loud
With its plans and intentions
For me to achieve
The world is loud
With its good and its bad
Its right and its wrong
It's all figured out
Can't you see who to be?
But something inside
Quite small and afraid
Says that's not it
Not a pathway for me
But the voice is so small…
How can that be?

Embracing Your Joy

In the early stages of discovering your authentic self expression and purpose, like me, you may not enjoy ALL the aspects of the opportunities available to you at any given moment. However, I urge you to make the choices that provide the greatest likelihood or probability that the experience it offers (the people, the places, the conversations and words you use, the ideas, the actions, the impact and results in the world, the overall environment you are in, and as well as both the present and possible monetary rewards, etc.) will have at least SOME enjoyable aspect(s) for you. This is heeding the wise suggestion of Joseph Campbell to "follow your bliss." And as you do this, if you practice this time and time again, the fullness of your bliss will unfold over your lifetime like a beautiful flower coming into its own.

I want to further emphasize and support this notion of "following your bliss" and engaging activities where you experience the most joy.

> *Joy is life-force filled. And what people want most on this planet (including yourself) is life-force. The more you embody and become a channel for life-force energy, the more you become of SERVICE to others – you are giving them what they most want and need.*

This is the key to success. Becoming a channel for, and access to, what people want most: life-force energy. The most powerful way to do that is to follow your very own bliss. Isn't that divine?! And here's another reason to follow your bliss – when you do, you become more and more unstoppable. Another word for Joy, and for Bliss, is Inspiration. When you are inspired you are connected to the divine flow and intelligence of the Universe. Your personal energy is optimized, solutions and ideas come to you "from beyond" and your overall experience is amazing. When you are inspired, you have "spirit inside" – and when you have spirit-inside you bring spirit and life-force energy to others.

As a NexGen Human, you operate from your soul. That's really what we are talking about here. The person who operates from the soul and allows truth to flow *through* them, is inspired in the deepest sense. Such a man or woman is a rare and treasured gift for all of us. When an artist is touched by Spirit and creates something from that authentic place, we are all touched. It's like looking at something here in the physical world that came from and represents the beauty, mystery, and magic of the metaphysical world. This is the kind of experience and impact you, as a NexGen Human, aspire to create for yourself and for others.

Wherever there is success AND joy, there is inspiration.

You can have success, with no joy or inspiration. But you cannot have joy without success because joy in and of itself is success! So are you going for the success "hoping for the joy" or are you going for the joy hoping for the success? If success in a material sense is important to you, I suggest doing both. Follow your bliss with a plan for manifesting material success.

As a NexGen Human you allow your open hearted creation following Spirit. You are willing to say yes and trust that instinct and take that first step, and "begin walking into it."

Manifesting your authentic purpose is a long term partnership with Spirit that unfolds over time. You are the instrument that Universal Life Force Intelligence is playing. Mother Theresa said it this way: "We are all pencils in the hand of God writing love letters to the Universe." What is your love letter to the Universe? What does God want to write with you and your life? Only YOU know the answer.

Soul Power

The Soul is the ultimate guide and influence of your life, either consciously *or unconsciously.* This power is similar to, yet different from, the power of your subconscious beliefs (the SLBs discussed in Chapter V). Your subconscious beliefs are also powerful and mysterious in the sense that they affect your life, your actions, and the experiences you have, without your conscious awareness of them. The Soul is similar in that it (which is really you) holds a desire and a commitment for your life that *it will manifest.* Your small self mind may desire one thing, but your Soul is ultimately more powerful as the deep resonant energy in your being. The key is to open up to this Soul purpose, to this divine choice, intelligence, and being, that is far beyond and more powerful than your conscious mind. The challenge for the NexGen Human is distinguishing between subconscious belief patterns that are ready for transcendence, and the Soul-based unconscious intentions guiding and influencing your life.

You want to work with and <u>release</u> subconscious belief patterns that no longer serve you. And you want to work with and <u>embrace</u> Soul-based power, energy, and intentions.

There is Only One You

The story of your life is UNIQUE! It took me a long time to understand this. It's your job to be the instrument that you are – if everyone in the band is trying to play lead guitar, that doesn't make for a very good band. Some of the best music is comprised of intricate elements and it's that ping of the triangle at just the right moment that sends chills up your spine – one could say this is a very tiny boring instrument – but when honored for what it IS, and appropriately expressed, it's magical! The same is true for food. You may have a dish that is based on chicken, that's the main ingredient, the featured performer, but it's the inclusion of that one special herb, or that one unique spice, that transforms the dish from everyday normal to amazing, divine deliciousness! The human race is like this. You might be the lead guitar, or you might be the chicken – the main "spotlight" featured elements – but then again you might be the triangle or the special spice THAT MAKES ALL THE DIFFERENCE IN THE WORLD!

As a NexGen Human you have moved out of the mindset that you should be doing what others are doing. And, just as importantly, you've moved out of the mindset that what *you* are doing *others* should be doing. Just because you may be a NexGen Human, doesn't mean *everybody* should be one! Everyone has their own unique path and time.

> *As a NexGen Human you honor the unique life path of each and everyone – whether you understand it or not.*

We live in a community of many levels from the family, to the neighborhood, to the town, to the city, to the state, to the nation, to the planet. We all have a role in the functioning of the community, at one or many levels, and it's essential we each play our authentic, inspired role. And at the same time, allow others to play their role, ***whatever that may be and however that may look.***

My role is fundamentally one of minister – at the time of the writing of this book, I'm quite young at it, like the young Sequoia we read about

THE TONGUE

One of the most powerful stories I was ever told that helped me embrace my true, authentic life path and purpose I call "The Analogy of The Tongue." I know that may sound a little gross, but it is memorable.

A number of years ago a good friend of mine saw that I was struggling to really embrace who I was as a minister, an evolutionary advocate, or spiritual conduit – I didn't really know what it was or what was wanting to evolve through me at that time. In the model I had grown up in and the life I was living at that time, it didn't make any sense, I didn't have any context or precedence for it.

So he said this to me:

He asked me to name a food that I do not like. I told him eggplant. He said, "OK, why do you not like eggplant?" I said "Because it's gushy, mushy, usually gray in color, and has a paste-like taste to it. There is nothing about it for me to like." He said "Great. Now, what if I told you everybody else is eating it, would you then eat it?" I said, "A lot of other people do like and eat it, and I still do not eat it. Therefore, no." He said "OK, great. Now, what if I told you you should eat it, because it's good for you and it's the right thing to do. Then would you eat it? Might you like it then?" I said, "No, I

don't care what you say about it, I know I don't like it and don't want to eat it." He said, "Good."

He went on to say "Now, is this something you would purchase, prepare, and serve dinner guests?" And I said "No way. I would not serve them something I myself do not like. In fact, I wouldn't even know if it was good or not anyhow. So, no, I would not serve it to guests at my house for dinner." Then he said, "Is there anything I or anyone could do to make you like and eat eggplant?" I said "No, I just don't like it."

He said "Great. Your purpose in life is just like this. It's that simple. It's innate in you, just like your preferences for food are. You like some things and you don't like other things. Just like you won't try to like and eat eggplant because everyone else does, or because someone tells you you should, or because someone else asks for it, don't try to force yourself into some other life purpose! Eat and serve others what *you* know and like. Anything else is a disservice to yourself and others. It's not authentic!"

You have a tongue, or a taste, for your purpose, your own Authentic Creative Agenda. You've had it since you were born. If you are just willing to trust this, and you are willing to look, my bet is you will see it. If you are like me, you

> may be finding your "taste" by tasting many things you do not like. That's fine. The more you know what you don't like, the closer you are to discovering what you do like.

in Chapter VI – but my role is to fundamentally point toward, and facilitate, an experience of the Eternal Spirit in the lives others. To help others bring alive this aspect in *their* lives. That's my job. How do I know that? Because when I do that for myself, and for others, it brings me the most joy of anything I ever do! I am inspired – filled with Spirit inside – when I am doing this. I am inspired right now as I write this, because I am aligned with and am fulfilling my highest purpose and mission. Whether one person reads this or thousands read this, by allowing myself to be the instrument I am for the expression of Universal Life Force, Evolutionary Energy, I am fulfilled, and my life purpose is fulfilled. I can feel that and know that. And so can you, for yourself, *on your own unique mission* and life path.

> *Life Force Energy can be expressed and transmitted in an __infinite__ number of ways, the question is: What is YOUR way? Find that, embrace that, and I guarantee you will be more than happy.*

There is an old story that exemplifies this aspect of *being who you are* and the power that comes from it (please note I am paraphrasing this ancient story for illustration purposes). In an ancient town in India the Ganges River threatened to flood its banks and completely devastate the surrounding town. The King of this town went to the River God to plead for mercy and stop the flood. The River God said to the King, "Show me one person in your town who is living and expressing their authentic self and I will subside the river." So the King started searching for this person. He first presented his high-priest, and the River God said "No." Then he presented his top magistrate, and the River God said "No." Then he presented his top physician, and the River God said "No." Exasperated, the King put out word to the town that to save themselves from the impending flood they needed to present one person to the River God who was living their authentic life purpose. Person after person presented themselves, from all walks and disciplines, and to each the River God said "No." Until finally there was only one person left, the town prostitute, and while the King thought for sure she was not it, out of desperation he presented her to the River God, and the River God said "Yes." And the river subsided. She was the only one, including the King, in the whole town that was living their authentic life purpose.

I tell you this story because it illustrates two very important lessons when it comes to living *your* authentic life purpose: #1) don't judge your, or anyone else's, purpose, and #2) there is real power in living your authentic life purpose – you can save a town and stop a river from rising!

We've all experienced souls that are engaged in their most authentic and soul inspired mission. They come from all walks of life. From the janitor you see sweeping the halls with a knowing smile on his face, to the restaurant where the meals are cooked with love and are beyond delicious, to the musicians who bring a tear to your eye when they play, to the architect who creates a space inside which your soul feels free, to the attorney who compassionately helps you through and out of a mess, to the airline pilot who takes pride in transporting people safely and efficiently from city to city, to the elementary school teacher who treats each and every child with love and respect, to the 1,000's of people who go to work in 1,000's of roles with a smile on their face making their difference and contributing the essence of themselves and who they are.

HEALING FIRST

One very important thing to appreciate is the need to heal yourself first, before you'll be truly effective in living your life's purpose and serving the world. As we've seen in the preceding chapters of this book, especially chapter five *It's All About Evolution*, there is no one and no thing to transform, but yourself. You do your inner world work and I guarantee the outer world will take care of itself.

I'm bringing this up here in this chapter, *The Power of Your Purpose*, because I want you to know you will not be free to fully manifest your divine authentic life path and dreams UNTIL you've sufficiently healed yourself – your hurts and wounds, your places of anger and frustration, your internal beliefs about not being good enough, or not being smart enough, or not...whatever!

You can engage your dreams, and I wholeheartedly recommend that you do, but just know that until you've sufficiently re-integrated those lost parts of yourself, those parts of yourself you have rejected and hid away, and that you are more than likely not even aware of – your path will be more about inner world healing, and less about manifesting, or creating your dreams (try as you might), in the external physical world.

And this is totally fine, in fact it's great! Because as we know, again from Chapter V, *It's All About Evolution* anyhow! So this is not time wasted. In fact it's some of the most honorable, valuable, and rewarding work you can do.

I didn't know this, in fact I didn't even know I had hurts and wounds to be healed they were so far stuffed down and out of my conscious awareness. I was thinking to myself, "what's all this fluffy, self indulgent crap about healing – lets get out there and create something." But as you engage your path, the world is your reflection, and if you're paying attention like I was, you'll begin to see areas where you're not so free, where you're not so happy, and where you're not so effective. These are your golden opportunities for personal healing, transformation, and evolution.

You can think of these internal emotional hurts and wounds in a literal, physical sense. Just like someone who's been shot and is bleeding, until you attend to the wound, stop the bleeding and facilitate the healing process, obviously your ability to live your life, manifest your dreams, and contribute and serve your fellow beings is severely limited.

Until you've done this healing work for yourself, everything else is like icing over mud – things may look pretty on the surface, but beneath it all and at the core is the true picture. Be willing to engage your own healing, this is a huge step on your hero's journey, and is the beginning of true access to the life of your dreams.

ALL WORK CAN BE SOUL WORK. It makes no difference WHAT you are doing. What matters is that it is <u>YOUR</u> WORK TO DO.

If you can find joy (or if joy finds you) in what you are doing, then the how will take care of itself! Joy can be found in ANY job, role, or life – but YOUR joy will only be found in YOUR unique life in the unique way YOU are meant to live and express it. This is the power of your purpose.

The NexGen Human's "7 Principles of Purpose"

As a conclusion to this very important chapter I want to summarize and present Seven Principles of Purpose and Seven Myths surrounding them:

Principle #1

You have a purpose. Each and every one of us does. We are born with it. Others may have a similar purpose, but your methods of manifesting it and bringing it into the world for others are unique to you and you only.

Principle #2

It's your job to find it. No one else can do this for you no matter how much you may wish that someone else will "pull out your gifts" or "discover you." These are all victim based ways of being that avoid YOUR responsibility for YOUR life. Thank God that you and only you are in control of your life. That is a gift; it is divine design. So while at first this may seem like a burden, once you engage in discovering your purpose, you'll be very glad it's all up to you.

Principle #3

90% + of the people out there don't care or don't want what you have to offer. BUT (and this is a HUGE but), BUT about 10% do! This is a major downfall for most people stepping out on their true life purpose – they share who they are with those closest to them (because who else would they share it with, right?) and those people are in the 90% who don't need or want THAT particular gift being offered (they can't recognize the value) and hence they believe since <u>they</u> don't want it, no one else probably does either. WRONG!

Here's an example – a Gold Record sells 1 million copies. If we look just at the United States where approximately 300 million people live, that means that 299 million people DID NOT buy the record! Yet this is an amazingly successful album and musician who is now well known and quite well off. If they made the same assumption that most of us make that "since the first few people I shared with did not like my stuff, then everyone is not going to like my stuff" they would never have gotten off the ground. This is simply a matter of marketing and reaching YOUR people and has nothing to do with the quality or value of your offering.

Unless you've talked with 100 people, I don't want to hear how "nobody likes or needs my stuff."

Principle #4

Your customers will not show up until you do. The 10% of people who want and need your stuff will not show up till YOU DO. You must show up first. You must stand up and say "This is who I am, this is what I have to offer, and if you want some, let's talk." Think about it, do you ever buy anything from someone, or from a company, without them first coming to you? Rarely, if ever does this happen. Usually, we see an advertisement, or someone makes a referral, or we find it on the internet. The point is, these people and products are already OUT THERE either finding you, or for you to find. They have "shown up" and said "this is what I am, this is what I have to offer, if you want some, let's talk." To employ Principle #4 that's what you've got to do as well.

Principle #5

You will be happy, successful and satisfied with your life to the extent you embrace your authentic purpose – AND – you will be unhappy, unfulfilled, dissatisfied and frustrated to the extent you do not. In fact, I would go so far as to say that we must create and manifest our life purpose or we will die. Ultimately we do die, and lives best lived have exhausted their life purpose and are ready for transition. However, those people resisting their life purpose will end up making themselves sick, they are literally "killing themselves" because they are not on purpose expressing and channeling Life Force in the way they themselves have already chosen (and, yes, suffering can actually be a part of one's authentic life path, it was for me). As harsh as this may sound, it's actually preferable to be dead, than alive and resisting your purpose. For if you are not here doing what you've come here to do, why hang around? To the extent you've buried and resisted your purpose, it does *appear* at some point to be easier to exit the game and start over. However, the fact you are reading this book, means you now know whatever you are experiencing IS PART OF YOUR LIFE PATH AND PURPOSE, and it's your job to see just exactly how this all fits together and makes sense for you, in your life.

Consider that perhaps your life purpose was chosen before you were born. Even if that's true, you still have a choice in this life. That choice is whether you will embrace your purpose, or resist your purpose. Partner with Universal Life Force Energy, or block and resist it. It's up to you. But just know that you will be happy, successful and satisfied with your life to the extent you embrace your authentic purpose – AND – you will be unhappy, unfulfilled, dissatisfied and frustrated to the extent you do not.

Principle #6

It's not your job to question your purpose; it's your job to engage and live it. Given the reality you may find yourself in when you discover your authentic purpose, your purpose may seem ridiculous, unimportant, impossible, or perhaps "not for you." But this is a destiny pre-chosen for you, most likely even by you, for your life, and it cannot be changed. And resistance, as we've seen with Principle #5, is futile. The sooner you get on board and embrace your purpose, the happier you'll be. Damn the torpedoes, full speed ahead!

Principle #7

You must nurture your purpose. Your purpose will ebb and flow throughout the course of your life, at times strong, at others weak, and even at times impossible to distinguish. But through it all is YOU, and your job is to continually nurture your purpose, keep fanning the flames (that will never go out) and know that it is your job to build the bridge from the unmanifest (metaphysical) to the manifest (physical). To make your vision a reality, here, and now. That is the game.

Some Myths & Realities

In addition to these seven underlying Principles of Purpose, there are seven major myths surrounding life purpose. Let's debunk these myths right here and free you from their burden:

Myth #1: It's too late for me – or – I'm too old and missed my chance.
Reality: It's NEVER too late. If you're still here, you are here for a reason (nothing exists without one) and you got time – get on with it.

Myth #2: Leap and "my wings will grow" on the way down – or – Leap and a net will appear.
Reality: Plan, plan, and plan, then leap and GROW YOUR WINGS on the way down. Do not expect them to grow by themselves, they won't. With regards to the net, put your own net there, then leap. Again, don't expect one to magically appear for you – better to put it there yourself.

Myth #3: Do what you love and the money will follow.
Reality: No it won't. If that happens for some people, it's out of pure luck, because this is NOT a law. Manifesting money, like manifesting

anything else in life, requires focus and competence. Even if you plan to manifest money out of the "illusion" you are living in, you will still have to do the work of transforming your limiting beliefs that this is not possible (note: if you truly believed it was possible, it would already have happened for you). To the extent you focus on manifesting money and build your competence in that arena (or release limiting beliefs you have about how it is created), while at the same time doing what you love, it's quite likely that money will flow from your efforts.

Myth #4: You can be anything you want.

Reality: No you can't. Please avoid torturing yourself with this fallacy. While there is a relatively wide range of creative roles you can engage on your authentic life path, you have a specific purpose and a unique mission in life. The Universe has a plan for you – recognize and embrace it – that's your access to the life of fulfillment you so desire.

Myth #5: The purpose of life is material success – or – if one is successful in the material area of life, then they are successful in all areas of life.

Reality: The purpose of life is spiritual evolution, the constant expansion of your capabilities to be and manifest who you are. This is typically achieved by overcoming adversity and challenge, barriers both real and perceived. Manifesting material goods is only ONE aspect of the challenge. People who are good at that may or may not be evolving spiritually. In other words, we can expand our bank accounts without expanding who we are in other areas.

Myth #6: You need formal education, training, and credentials to make a difference.

Reality: You need *competence* to make a difference. Competence is developed and obtained in many ways – of which formal education and training is only one. In addition, when you are on your authentic purpose, you do not need "others" to validate you. *If you have truly done your work* to become the open channel for life force you are meant to be, then the Universe is your credentials and authority, and others will instinctively know that. People will *get* that your power comes from the Universe, NOT from external credentials, or a few letters after your name. God, Universal Intelligence, Great Spirit, Source is the most powerful credential there is – align with God, give your life over to "him," and others will intuitively know where you are coming from (authentic Life Force Energy will be flowing).

Myth #7: If anything is going to happen, it's up to <u>me</u> to make it happen.

Reality: Non-local intelligence has infinite organizing power and can make things happen far beyond what our little physical selves may be able to think about, much less orchestrate. The Universe will make things happen IF the local intent/desire is aligned (authentic) with it, i.e. the clarity of the local channel will determine the efficiency of the non-local power. Your job is to maximize the clarity of the local channel (get your self, small "s," out of the way) and make room for non-local intelligence and power to express through you.

QUESTIONS FOR REFLECTION

+ Do you feel you are on your authentic life path fulfilling your unique mission? If no, what do you think your unique mission might be? (Note: typically the first thing, right there for you, is it. You can also ask yourself "If I did know, what would I say it is?")

+ What people in your life do you really admire? Notice what it is about them you admire and know you can only see in others what is already present in you.

Opportunities for Action

+ Do something in the next week that truly brings you joy.
+ Look back over all the experiences in your life and see if you can identify your "Theme of Power" - the common thread through all those experiences that attracted you to them in the first place. What is the common "thread of joy" that you loved about each of these roles and experiences in your life? These are huge clues to your life purpose.
+ Contact me at Roger@GoBeyondBelief.com to take The Passion Test® and get on track fulfilling your destiny.

Powerful Resources

+ Book: "Liberating Everyday Genius: A Revolutionary Guide for Identifying and Mastering YOUR Exceptional Gifts" by Mary-Elaine Jacobsen, Psy.D. – this is an amazing book that provides a new perspective on the emerging capacities arising in ourselves, in the human race, at this point in time. A critical contribution of this work is her distinction of Evolutionary Intelligence or "EvI" for short. Her formula for Evolutionary Intelligence is "EvI = MI + GT + AD" which says Evolutionary Intelligence is the sum of one's Multiple Intelligences (MI) plus their Gifted Traits (GT) plus their Advanced Development (AD). She provides a test you can take to measure your level of these three areas and hence determine your "level" of EvI. This is a <u>must have</u> book for NexGen Humans and will help you better understand your place in the evolutionary picture.

+ Book: "The Type-Z Guide to Success – A Lazy Person's Manifesto for Wealth and Fulfillment" by Marc Allen – I can't say enough about this book and the new paradigm for success that Marc presents. Marc is living proof that one can live the life of their dreams and not "suffer, sacrifice, and work hard" to achieve it. Our society is dominated by Type A personalities and it is *believed* that the only way to achieve your dreams and succeed in life is through long hours of hard work, sacrifice, and suffering. While this may be the right and authentic path for some people (Type A's) it is totally inauthentic for many others – meaning it goes against every bone in your body to live your life that way. Marc's main message is overwhelmingly "To thine own self be true" – follow <u>your</u> bliss and trust in <u>your</u> higher power. Yes there is effort involved in achieving your dreams, but it can be done in balance with *joy and ease* – listen to Marc, he has it mastered.

+ Book: "The Passion Test – The Effortless Path to Discovering Your Destiny" by Janet Bray Attwood and Chris Attwood. When I first took The Passion Test I thought I knew what I was here to do. However by following the process led by Janet and Chris I discovered some major things that shifted how I looked at my life and my priorities for living. This is such an important and effective process I became a Certified Passion Test Facilitator and have integrated this work into Beyond Belief. Besides providing a tool to ensure all NexGen Humans are clear on their mission and can stay focused on it over time, the work of Chris and Janet provides powerful distinctions for living your passions each and every day. Living from your passions is not a "normal" life (it's far more exciting!) and there are skills and ways of being in the world that

Chris and Janet have brought forward. As a Certified Passion Test Facilitator I am trained to lead people through the entire process and support them to develop these skills and live a passionate life. Visit my website www.GoBeyondBelief.com for more information on The Passion Test.

+ Book: "Conscious Evolution – Awakening the Power of Our Social Potential" by Barbara Marx Hubbard. I was blown away when I first read this book! It put so much of what I was experiencing into context and provided powerful insights into "just what the heck is going on here?" One of the most potent metaphors in this book has to do with what are called imaginal cells that play a key role in the metamorphosis of the caterpillar. We are all familiar with the age old metaphor of the "caterpillar transformed into a butterfly," but Barbara takes it a step further and goes *inside* the process showing us what is going on in the cocoon. "When the caterpillar weaves its cocoon, imaginal disks begin to appear. These disks embody the blueprint of the butterfly yet to come. Although the disks are a natural part of the caterpillar's evolution, its immune system recognizes them as foreign and tries to destroy them. As the disks arrive faster and begin to link up, the caterpillar's immune system breaks down and its body begins to disintegrate. When the disks mature and become imaginal cells, they form themselves into a new pattern, thus transforming the disintegrated body of the caterpillar into the butterfly." NexGen Human. Imaginal Cell. Very interesting.

Chapter VIII

Partnership with Source

There's an old saying:

> *"The longest journey a person will ever take*
> *is from their head to their heart."*

This has certainly been true in my experience.

It has only been relatively recently that I have developed my <u>skill</u> to consistently live from my heart. And, oh what a difference it makes! Living from the heart has been nothing less than a complete and total transformation of my experience of being alive. I have come to realize that as much as the head wants to run the show, "I" do best when my head serves my heart.

Our Focus on the Head

This discovery of the heart is a revelation at this time in history more than at any other time because in our modern western civilization we have systematically disconnected our "selves" from our hearts and bodies. Through schooling we have overemphasized the development of our intellect while *neglecting* our heart and body-based wisdom. Usually the first programs to get cut in educational curriculums are the touchy-feely courses of art and music – the very place where some of our non-head-based skills might actually have a chance of being developed. However, even in these classes, all too often the intellect wins out and linear, systematic guidelines rule the process and experience. For example, music is typically not "created," rather it is produced (as in a production line) from pre-written music year in and year out using the same processes with simply new students each year. And art is boiled down to "making something," whether a picture or a ceramic mug. And Physical Education – another program likely to be hit with cuts – has little to do with the mind-body connection. Rather, it's focus is on developing the body as simply a carrier for the intellect and the mind. We stay in shape so the body doesn't distract us (with health problems and issues) from our primary goal of developing and using the head-based intellect. And on, and on, it goes, all the way up through college and advanced education. Education is evolving, but traditionally it's been very focused on the head.

This training, experience, and head-based way of being is continued on into the work place. The modern corporation is what the schooling process is designed to serve – producing "thinkers" that "get things done." This is fine if thinking and getting things done is what life is all about. And don't get me wrong, I like thinking and getting things done! The problem is, that is only one part of life, and is only one part of who we are as human beings. So by default, and by training, we are leaving a huge part (and perhaps the most important part) of ourselves outside at the door of the institutions within which much of our society is spending most of it's waking hours. Besides being a HUGE missed opportunity for employers, it's the employee that really ends up paying the price (we've all seen the statistics on the very high level of worker dissatisfaction in the American workplace).

In most corporations there is very little room for the heart – and the full power of a human being - since everything must be explained in a black and white, linear, and extremely logical manner that very clearly supports the bottom line. In this type of environment employees must consistently sacrifice their true feelings and "toe the corporate line" or risk extrication – keep your head below the mow line or risk getting it cut off. This cumulative corporate wounding of the soul (as a good friend of mine calls it) takes its toll and results in dead to life employees, or a bunch of "corpses" in the "corpse-oration," as Robert Kiyosaki, author of *Rich Dad Poor Dad* has called it. You can walk in the majority of companies today and immediately see and *feel* this phenomenon. People have sacrificed the biggest, most powerful part of themselves – their heart and soul - to fit in and survive.

Even religion has been *intellectualized*. The religious *experience* has been fundamentally removed and everything has been taken literally. In today's religion, although it is transforming, the goal is to *understand* as much as possible (a mind-based process) and take everything else on "faith" – since as previously mentioned, if you have no experience of something for yourself, you must take its existence on faith. And faith is based in belief, which again is a mind-based process. Even the definition of religion has *belief* built in to it. From the Webster's New World Dictionary: "Religion - **belief** in or worship of God or gods."

Don't Ever Leave Me!

On the path of the NexGen Human it's quite likely you'll experience many moments of epiphany and enlightenment. These are fabulous moments and times in one's life. One that I'd like to share with you from my life was particularly impactful because I received some insight that has really made a difference for me in my day-to-day life. I'm hoping it will make a difference for you too.

At this particular time in my life I was working very hard in a corporate role with a lot of responsibility. I had planned in a 4 day silent retreat on the Big Sur Coast of California. I had reservations at a hermitage down there and I was going to spend three nights and four full days in silence; both in solitude and with the Christian monks that are in residence there. I had never done anything like that before and I didn't know what to expect, but I was looking forward to it.

So I headed on down there, checked in, got to my trailer, and set up shop. I had taken only the basics: a couple books, my journal, and some warm clothes since it can get quite cold and foggy. While I brought my computer and cell phone, I purposely left them turned off and in the car – if I was going to do this thing I wasn't going to cheat myself out of the experience by doing stuff I was always doing.

Given the high-speed mode I had been running in, it took a little while to settle into the energy and rhythm of the place. If you've never been there, the Big Sur coast is one of the most spectacular and powerful places on the planet and I highly recommend you visit. On about the second or third day I decided to go on a walk down the winding, mile long driveway that connects the hermitage to Highway 1 that runs along the ocean. The hermitage sits high on the mountainside overlooking a huge expanse of the Pacific Ocean.

As I was walking down this road I just started becoming more and more open to everything that was around me. The flowers that were blooming were brighter than I would normally see them. The trees and the birds and everything was just coming into my awareness at a more intense level, and it kept unfolding that way as I continued down the path. It was the most amazing experience. I even wrote a short poem after this experience called "Look At That, Wow!" because everything I looked at was a Wow! experience. It was that impressive, it was amazing.

Eventually I came to this one particular bend in the road where there was a rock outcropping. As I stepped out onto that outcropping, I was just grounded there on that solid piece of earth. From there, the spectacular Big Sur coastline unfolded and laid out to my left as far as my eyes could see. And out in front of me was the Pacific Ocean going out as far as I could see, gleaming in the sunshine. And above me was the sky, huge and abundant, with these little white clouds floating in it. And I just stood there on that rock. And my heart broke wide open. I couldn't contain the emotion I was experiencing, the love was just pouring down though me. That's the best way I can describe it. I just opened up in that moment and had that experience of oneness. That everything is fine. Everything is OK. I have a place in the Universe. And this is it. There is nothing to do. No where to go. Everything is whole and complete, right here, right now.

At that moment I was so FULFILLED and so connected to the energy of the Universe that I yelled out "Don't ever leave me!" And what I instantly heard back was "We can't. Only you can leave us." And I started laughing, because in that moment it was so blatantly obvious to me that indeed, it's ME that is coming & going, connecting & disconnecting. I am in the driver's seat and I am choosing. Just like you are. It or They, or however you want to contextualize it for you in your experience - Universal Intelligence, Great Spirit, Source, God Energy —is always there. And it's us that is moving in and out of connection with It.

As a NexGen Human you are Going Beyond Belief,
to KNOWING the presence and existence
of an intelligence larger and greater
than your small separate self (intellectual, thinking mind).
As a NexGen Human you access and align with an intelligence that is
at the same time both inside and outside of you, an intelligence that is
beautiful, loving, and always available.

When you are truly connected to this Source Energy and the abundance of Love that *it* is, you are so full and satisfied, you need nothing else. Nothing is missing. You are fully-realized, whole and complete, at one and present with all that is. And it's a paradox that <u>from this fullness, this whole and completeness, your inspiration for creating will flow.</u> The mind does not understand this. You see, the mind thinks there has to be problems, frustration, pain, and suffering *in order to* be motivated enough to do something about it. "Frustration is the mother of invention," right? Not necessarily. This may just be more fear-based *thinking*.

As a NexGen Human you connect with Source, and from that place of fullness, you allow divine inspiration to flow and move you to create.

Through our modern societal systems we have become a civilization of people walking around with our awareness pretty much focused from the neck up, completely disconnected from the power and wisdom of our body, and especially our hearts. These years and years of experiences have resulted in an intense *conditioning*, that has real physiological implications that produce habitual ways of being, living, and experiencing the world, if you can even call it an experience. We have learned to *think* about the world, analyze and manipulate it, rather than *be in it*. This habitual way of *being* produces an experience of separation, a view that holds: "I am here, and the world is out there." And since the world is "out there separate from me" what there is to do is analyze it, try to understand it, judge it, and try to control and manipulate it. All this to ensure my survival, satisfy my needs, minimize my suffering, and maximize my pleasurable experiences.

We have been conditioned out of our bodies and into our heads, where we have been stuck, wondering why life is not more rich. We *sense* life could be more beautiful and yet cannot think our way into making it so. While thinking as a process certainly can be valuable, <u>thinking *about* life is the booby prize</u>! John Lennon is known for saying "Life is what happens to you while you are making other plans." What I hear him saying here is that, since planning is a head-based activity, while you are busily *thinking about* and *planning* your life, you completely miss the actual experience of it.

Something more powerful than head-based planning and thinking is taking place.

You Have a Choice

Long ago, back in my college days, I attended an open Campus Christians Club meeting. As I settled into the presentation I saw an overhead slide of an image that has never left me. The presenter was illustrating how most people live their lives with themselves at the center, and how, on the other hand, living the Christian life is a choice to put God at the center. The image was one of a cross at the center of a life with various life activities surrounding it. While the word "God" as well as the image of the cross did not specifically call to me, the <u>concept</u> being presented certainly did. It was about serving and living life for something larger and higher than your "self" (small "s"). I left the meeting without joining the club, but that image and concept had been forever impressed upon me.

As I reflect on my journey from the head to the heart, I realize it is much like this traditional religious concept portrayed at that meeting. Through the heart you can access WISDOM, far beyond what your head alone can access (in fact, I may go so far as to say that no true WISDOM

ACCESS TO WISDOM

I n this chapter we are talking about establishing a strong partnership with God, Universal Intelligence, Great Spirit, or Source – which is THE critical skill to survive and thrive in the 21st century. While Spirit communicates with us in many ways, one of the most powerful and effective ways I have found to partner with the power of the Universe, is to tune into my own body. If it's true that we and Great Spirit are one, then we need look no further than right here, right where we are, to tap into divine intelligence and guidance.

In our western paradigm of living, we are accustomed to *thinking* of intelligence arising, or coming from, the head. Familiar terms like "Use your head" and "Get your head in the game," exemplify this way of thinking. However, what science has discovered in recent years is that intelligence actually exists all over the body – and that in fact there are neurons, similar to those in our brain, that exist in the heart and as well in the stomach. The new field of neuro-cardiology has called this bundle of neurons in the heart the heart-brain.

Studies have shown that there is more communication going from the heart to the brain, than from the brain to the heart. The brain does not run the heart – in fact, in a fetus, the heart is formed and starts pumping before the brain is formed. And if you know anything about heart-transplants, you'll know that a heart removed from the body can continue to beat with no connection to the brain. There are also neurons in the gut – we're all familiar with "gut instinct" – but we haven't really understood it until now. So there is wisdom, insight, and intelligence that we can access from other parts of ourselves, however we have to pay attention, and this is the key.

As we've seen, the head is so dominant with its screaming and yelling and nonstop fear based messages, that the subtle aspects of ourselves get drowned out and you just can't hear them. Think of the mind, or your head, as the manager, and think of your body, and especially your heart, as the leader, as the visionary. Without a divinely developed vision, the manager, or your head, is just spinning its wheels doing busy work. Your mind is there to serve your heart, however most people are so in their mind, and disconnected from their body-based wisdom, that the mind is <u>dysfunctionally</u> running the show.

As a NexGen Human you want to get connected to your body and access ALL your wisdom.

arises from the head at all!).

When living from the heart there is a tangible experience
of being guided by and serving something far larger than your self
(small "s").

This wisdom could be called God, Universal Intelligence, Infinite Intelligence, Great Spirit, or Source. Ultimately it cannot be labeled. Nonetheless we can have a direct EXPERIENCE of it....through the heart, and the *entire* body itself.

OUR VIEW OF GOD

On Tuesday, September 12, 2006, *USA Today* ran an article about a study performed by sociologists at Baylor University. This study surveyed 1,721 Americans and was undertaken to create a better understanding of our nation's view of God. The first paragraph of this article read "The United States calls itself one nation under God, but Americans don't all have the same image of the Almighty in mind." Though 91.8% of those surveyed indicated they believe in God, a higher power, or a cosmic force, they had four distinct views of God's personality and engagement in human affairs. These four Gods were dubbed by the researchers as Authoritarian, Benevolent, Critical, or Distant. The following highlights from the study (as mentioned in the USA Today article) are quite interesting and revealing regarding where we are as a people in our evolving understanding, views, and perceptions of "God":

+ The Authoritarian God (31.4% of respondents) is angry at humanity's sins and engaged in every creature's life and world affairs. He is ready to throw the thunderbolt of judgment down on "the unfaithful or ungodly."

139

- The Benevolent God (23%) still sets absolute standards for mankind in the Bible. More than half (of these respondents) want the government to advocate Christian values. This group sees primarily a forgiving God, more like the biblical father who embraces his prodigal son.

- The Critical God (16%) has his judgmental eye on the world, but he's not going to intervene, either to punish or to comfort. This group has very traditional beliefs, yet they're less inclined to go to church or affiliate seriously with religious groups. They are less inclined to see God as active in the world.

- The Distant God (24.4%) is "no bearded old man in the sky raining down his opinions on us." They see this God as a cosmic force that launched the world, then left it spinning on its own.

(Note: these four visions of God are not mutually exclusive and they don't include the 5.2% of Americans who say they are atheists. Rounding out the percentages are people who didn't answer or who were unsure).

As I read this article what struck me most was the sense of separation (from God) apparent in each of these four views. In each one there is a God, and there is a me and/or a world, and this God is doing things to me and the world, or not doing things to me and world, based on what I believe to be true.

Setting aside the parent-child models of relationship being played out in each of these views, if you've read the previous chapters of this book (especially chapters IV and V, "The Great Transformation," and "It's All About Evolution," respectively) and if you look closely at these four mainstream views of God, you will recognize the ego/small self present in these views. Remember the ego, or our small self, sees itself as separate and alone with survival as the primary objective. The ego also plays the victim role and is therefore not responsible for the things "God" is doing to me, or by extension, to the world. Hmmm. Now, the important thing to notice is how this <u>belief</u> significantly limits the individual power of each person subscribing to it. It does this by separating the self from God (Universal Intelligence, Great Spirit, Source), and in so doing creating one as a victim of this external all powerful God – true even of those subscribing to The Distant God, since they are victims of his/her neglectful non-presence.

Historical/Traditional/Religious View of "Human–God" Relationship

GOD

Rewarded or punished based on behavior...

Human

...with Heaven and Hell as the ultimate Carrot and Stick

This study gives us an idea of where the American culture and our cultural conversation is at this present moment in time. This is partially why mainstream media is disempowering for a NexGen Human – because 90%+ of it is reflecting and reinforcing these traditional perspectives. YOU are wanting to EVOLVE (beyond these historical and limiting belief systems), however, the challenge is finding the reinforcing and "evolutionary friendly" places where you can interact with others of like mind.

Remember, the Hero's Journey of the 21st Century is from Isolation to Integration, from Poor Suffering Bastard to Divinely Inspired Being. Along the way one's view of God transforms from an *external* concept to an *internal* reality. On this journey, the illusion of separation is transcended as you open your heart to a divine and amazing partnership with Source. This I would say, is a view of God that was not specifically distinguished in the Baylor study. Perhaps we can call this "View Number 5," or "The Integral View", or perhaps even "The NexGen Human View."

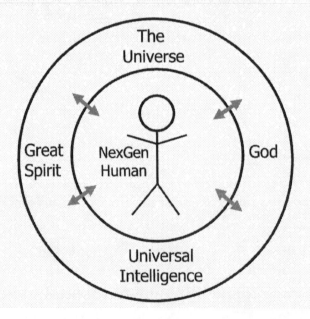

"NexGen Human–God" Relationship

*It is the simple man that expects to see **God** outside himself.*

A final important distinction to recognize is that you are not God, just like your hand is not you. You are <u>part</u> of God/Universal Intelligence/ Great Spirit/Source, just like your hand is part of you. It would be incorrect to say "I am God," just like it would be incorrect to say that you are your hand. You are much more than your hand alone, and God is much more than you alone. However, the two are inextricably linked. And it's the integral partnership of the two that serves the highest purpose and fulfillment that we are interested in.

Making the Transition

As I transitioned to living more from my heart than my head, I experienced just how loud and dominating the messages, thoughts, and voices from my head can be – and how quiet and unassuming those from the heart can be. No wonder most of us don't live from the heart - with the head screaming so loudly you can hardly hear it!

The head is loud because its job is survival.
It perceives everything as a threat
and must therefore, absolutely, get your attention!

Because as far as it can tell, in its isolated, separated view of the world, if you don't do what it says, you will die (or at least something bad will happen)! Listen to your head-based messages closely and I think you will find most of the messages will have fear *of something bad happening* as their motive for action.

These can be big fears or small fears. In an earlier chapter, we considered getting to work on time as an example. Most people get out of bed and get to work on time to avoid a negative consequence. Acting out of a fear that "something bad will happen" is a sure sign your actions are coming from the head. The fears may be of something as small as a look of disapproval from a coworker, or something as large as a notice of termination for tardiness. Being motivated by this fear may get you to work on time, but your experience in the process is not one of choice – "you" are being run by a fear-based machine, worried about what will happen if you don't do what it says. Just take a look at what your experience is like when your actions are based in this fear – are you waking up with a sense of joy, purpose, and excitement for the day? Or are you more tired, grumpy, rushed, and *thinking* about all the things you *have to do* that day? Just look and make a note. The problem with living from the head all the time is your life experience is based on, and is all about, FEAR and avoidance of bad things happening. Which sucks (to put it bluntly) *even if you avoid those bad things happening!*

There is another way. And that way is the heart. As I was learning to live from my heart, and experiencing challenges in doing so, my coach had me stop and check in with my heart on what the root of the challenge was. As I connected with my heart and asked this simple question, its response was "Go ahead and listen to your head. Then stop, and take the few moments it takes to settle down and listen to *me*. After listening to both, then choose which path to follow and action to take." Like most heart-based wisdom, this made total sense! And it's exactly what I do.

The head will dominate you with fear, but living from the heart (like putting God, Great Spirit, or Universal Intelligence at the center of your life) is a CHOICE you make.

God/Universal Intelligence/Great Spirit/Source will never dominate or force you to do anything. Partnering with the Power of the Universe is a CHOICE YOU MAKE that doesn't happen automatically. Being run by your head happens automatically and is <u>not</u> a choice. This is the <u>default</u>. I cannot overemphasize this point: Being run by your head happens automatically and is NOT a choice. Living from your heart is a CHOICE YOU MAKE – and one that you will make over, and over, and over again….until it becomes a habit.

When you live from your heart, your life experience becomes based in trust, love, and creation (rather than fear, control, and survival). These two experiences are completely different universes. And as you practice living from your heart, seeing the magical results it produces and how amazing you feel, your mind tends to relax a bit. It still has its job to do, but as the voice of your heart gets stronger, the voice from your head will tone down a bit.

My Beloved

Hello my beloved
I have come for you
As you have come for me
Together we are Love
Your inner and outer beauty
Excites me and inspires me
You energize that part of me
That sometimes feels afraid
But in your loving kindness
That fear can melt away

And what is left my dear
Is love that's here to stay

The HeartMath® System

I would be totally remiss if at this point I did not mention HOW I finally made the transition to living from my heart. Over about 5 years *HeartMath* kept popping up in my world, however I never engaged it. But as they say "When the student is ready...." Well I must finally have been ready because it came into my world in a very big way. The Institute of HeartMath has developed the most reliable, repeatable, research-based SYSTEM of tools and processes that bring heart intelligence alive in day-to-day life. Because of its impact in transforming my life, I became a Licensed HeartMath® Provider to deliver their 1-on-1 coaching programs and bring the power of Heart Intelligence alive in life for others. Many people and programs *talk about* coming from the heart, but no one provides a tried and true SYSTEM of tools and processes that have been proven to work in day-to-day life, for anybody, at anytime, anywhere. HeartMath is truly unique and amazing in this regard (HeartMath is a registered trademark of the Institute of HeartMath. See the resource list at the end of this chapter for more information).

Your Infinite Nature

What we are really talking about here is access to, and realization of, the infinite nature of your Self (big "S").

You are an infinite being. And there is a part of you, your true eternal self, that is forever.

When you are connected to this part of yourself you do not fear death because you <u>realize</u> death is only the end of that which is finite. From this place of awareness death is simply a transition that, like all endings, also contains a beginning.

YOU, that deep and powerful you – that you know is there – never dies.

Another word for infinite is timeless. YOU are timeless. You can see the timeless nature of your Self when you realize that TIME itself does not exist, that time is a construct of the MIND. There is no past and there is no future. There is ONLY this present moment. Take a look at this in your own life – notice how the future always seems to somehow dissolve into the present! Notice this – we NEVER get to the future! We actually aren't *going* anywhere – we are here now, and now, and now. And that's it! And this is also true of your eternal self – it is timeless – and does not live and die, but is forever now.

As I was grappling with this concept of time in my life – actually more like struggling to be present - I was doing regular Zazen sittings with a Zen teacher. I asked her about this concept of time, being present and how to regard the future. I've never forgotten what she said. She shared with me some wisdom passed down to her from her teacher who said: "Stay in the present with an eye toward the future." This made total sense to me.

Another perspective on this paradox of being fully present yet creating a future or a "not yet realized present moment" came from Dr. Will Joel Friedman, a master of being in the present moment. Dr. Friedman introduced me to the concept of a "Present Tense Vision." A Present Tense Vision is a vision of what's possible with one very important distinction.

147

Rather than vision a possible future as "out there, someday soon, I will have this," a Present Tense Vision is fully experienced in the moment as the <u>vision</u> that it is. From this vision <u>you are having in the present moment</u> you take actions aligned with it, also in the present moment. In all of this you are living fully in each and every present moment without sacrificing a thing for something someday, maybe in the future. Rather, you have the vision in the present moment and take inspired actions also in the present moment. Pretty cool.

So be FREE in this knowing of your infinite, timeless, eternal nature. Be FREE to inhabit your wonderful BODY in each and every present moment and dance and create – for this is ITS purpose. And use your MIND – being careful to not let it use you.

YOU are an infinite being.

This is the KEY step where as a NexGen Human <u>you actually transform the idea of God from an external concept to an internal reality.</u> This is a choice you make. You are no longer looking to someone else to tell you what to do or to take care of you. You take responsibility for your own life and create your own unique connection to Source. You create <u>your own</u> compass, and <u>that</u> becomes the tool YOU GUIDE YOURSELF with.

Questions for Reflection

+ What historical beliefs of God have you had, and might you still have, that you are ready to *transcend and include* and release on your path of evolution?

✦ How does God/Great Spirit/Universal Intelligence/Source speak to you now? Where does divine guidance and inspiration come from in your life at this time?

Opportunities for Action

✦ Visit a place that for you is very inspiring – it might be the mountains, a lake, the ocean, the desert, looking up into the sky at night, or your very own backyard garden – go there and just sit in the silence and practice opening up your senses to the powerful energies of the Universe all around you. Take a journal to capture the insights and experiences that arise in your awareness.

Powerful Resources

✦ "Resources for Understanding the Quantum World" – Free Report, www.GoBeyondBelief.com. This is a free report I put together that is available on my website. Simply subscribe to my free "NexGen Human Newsletter" and you can download this report; it contains short descriptions of various resources that can help you better understand the scientific side of spiritual exploration. As Quantum Physicist Dr. John Hagelin, a leader in Unified Field Theory, has said "At the bottom of it all is the Unified Field, Intelligent Life Force Energy itself." How this is distinct from God is yet to be discovered, but for now they certainly seem the same to me. Developing your intellectual understanding of what Source is can be an important aspect of establishing your Partnership with Source. This was true for me – as a formally trained left brained engineer and businessman – and it may be for you as well. Note that some people have such a strong connection with and experience of Source Energy they don't need science to tell them that it exists. However, I would say they are the exception to the rule at this point in our evolution. Hence, we have modern day science which is doing a tremendous job of analyzing, experimenting with, and even quantifying metaphysical aspects of the Universe. This free report presents a collection of those resources I have found especially helpful in developing this understanding.

+ Beyond Belief Audio Program: Journey to Source and Vision Quest www.GoBeyondBelief.com/products.php - this is a very powerful program that facilitates a release of all the things that typically get in the way of experiencing our infinite nature. Through a relaxing and gentle process, you will release these things one by one and clear the way to experience the very Source of your being.

+ HeartMath® Voyage to Heart Intelligence – The Institute of HeartMath realized the best way to bring alive the heart's intelligence in life is by engaging a personalized process, with a trained professional, over time. The Voyage to Heart Intelligence is a structured program engaged in day-to-day, real-world life. The program is done over the course of six to eight weeks and includes one-on-one coaching, a powerful workbook, and even specialized music. This program will "teach you to fish," connecting you to the wisdom of your heart for the rest of your life. Visit www.GoBeyondBelief.com/coaching.php and/or contact me at Roger@GoBeyondBelief.com to get your Voyage started!

+ "Science of Mind – A Guide for Spiritual Living" – this is an amazing monthly magazine filled with positive thoughts, ideas, and concepts, based on the teachings of founder Ernest Holmes that embraces all paths and traditions of wisdom. The Science of Mind principles are further shared through the member churches of the United Church of Religious Science/United Centers for Spiritual Living. I look forward each month to the Daily Guides to Richer Living published in this magazine. Visit www.ScienceOfMind.com for more information and to subscribe to this publication.

* Book: "The Power of Now" by Eckart Tolle – this is one of the best books ever written when it comes to being in the present moment and experiencing "The Power of Now."

* Book: "The Direct Path – Creating a Journey to the Divine Using the World's Mystical Traditions" by Andrew Harvey. Andrew Harvey is an amazing speaker and spiritual leader. I've seen him several times, and once at a small gathering at a Church of Religious Science in Oakland, California, he spoke so powerfully he moved me to joyful tears multiple times as he activated Spirit in me and I resonated with the truth he was so powerfully presenting. I reference this book here not only because it is an amazing and rich integration of the world's mystical traditions and outlines a solid path to enlightenment, but mainly because it presents eighteen sacred practices for transformed spiritual living. All of which, if practiced honorably, will provide access to the Divine and further establish your Partnership with Source. Note that many of these eighteen practices are heart-based and as such are very compatible and aligned with HeartMath practices.

Chapter IX

Go with the Flow

The Time

You'll know when it's time.
You may think about in advance
Contemplate and wonder
But when The Time has come
The true and real time
You will know.
And action at that point is
Divine – it just is –
There is no force, control, or effort –
It is done –
Kingdom come thy will be done.
That is The Time.
Wisdom is allowing
All things to come
Into their own time
Trusting all things actually

> *Have their own time –*
> *We are stewards*
> *Of The Time*
> *More than creators, or makers*
> *Of The Time –*
> *We know –*
> *And by that mere fact*
> *It is divine.*
> *And so are we.*
> *Ahhh . . . The Time.*

This is a very important chapter and emerging competency of a NexGen Human. **Going with the flow** of life. We've all heard it a million times, but what does it really mean? And how good are you at actually going with the flow?

As a NexGen Human this skill, this competency, is a life long pursuit. It's a practice.

> *Going with the flow is not laziness*
> *or willy-nilly allowing just anything to happen.*
> *Going with the flow is an astute ability*
> *to walk the razors edge between action and non-action.*
> *Between doing and being.*
> *And integrating both.*

THE RIVER OF LIFE

A fabulous analogy is one of a river. Life, and the energies of life, flow along just like a river. And we, as human beings, are floating in this river of life. I like to think of myself in an inner-tube; it's more intimate than a boat, but not as strenuous as swimming. Now, floating along this river of life in your inner tube, you have several options: 1) you can paddle against the flow, 2) you can just float along, and 3) you can paddle with the flow (and actually there is another option – get out of the river – which we will address later in this chapter – but for now let's just focus on these three). Which of these three do you think is most productive? Well, you might say, it depends on what you are trying to do. Let's say you are interested in creating and having an experience of grace, ease, and efficiency; going as far along your river of life as possible with the least amount of effort. Which of these three options do you think is most likely to produce this result we are looking for? It's actually a combination of all three. If I were to recommend a ratio, I would say: 10% paddle against the river, 45% go with the flow, and 45% paddle with the river.

We can't simply paddle with the flow, because while this approach meets the objective of going as far along our river of life as possible, it requires effort and detracts from the first goal of having an experience of grace and ease. And while floating along definitely supports our intention of having an experience of grace and ease, we can't *only* float along because this does not support our intention of efficiency: going *as far along* the river of life as possible with the least amount of effort.

I'm recommending only 10% of the time paddling against the flow because you may over do number 3 (paddling with the flow) – getting too excited and overzealous, paddling away downstream, when suddenly you've propelled yourself right toward a rock. It's at these times a little back-paddling is appropriate to slow down a bit and correct your course. It also keeps things interesting. Note that paddling against the flow requires the most effort and is the most strenuous, and actually stops you from flowing down the stream. Given the power of the flow, however, it's unlikely you will actually go upstream, rather what happens is you stop moving – it's a holding pattern that requires a tremendous amount of effort to maintain. It's very tiring. And because it is very tiring, you will eventually start moving downstream anyhow, even though you may be back-paddling and trying to move upstream. This is truly wasted, unnecessary effort.

Most people's default ratio of river-navigating tactical deployment looks something like this: 60% paddling against the flow (the standard waking hours of getting things done in a stressed-out, forceful and rushed manner), 30% giving up and reluctantly going with the flow (crashing into bed, exhausted from paddling all day), and 10% actually paddling with the flow (seemingly random, coincidental experiences of grace and ease – when things seem to happen magically with incredibly little effort). And this ratio may be generous. Some people may spend their entire lives paddling against the flow, never even realizing there actually is a flow to their life they can partner with. Never realizing that even when they stop paddling, they are still moving along and down the stream of life. And never experiencing that incredible rush when you are aware of the flow, you're in the flow, and you are paddling with it, creating an unbelievable experience of grace and ease making incredible progress on your evolutionary journey of life.

In many spiritual traditions, water is representative of Spirit, or God, or the flow of Life Force energy. As a NexGen Human this is very appropriate.

The Ride of Your Life

Another metaphor for life is the roller coaster. I had a dream where I was observing an incredibly wild rollercoaster ride. It had individual cars traveling on it where typically one person, but as many as four people, could ride together (it did not have long trains of cars like most roller coasters have). And the track was full of big drops, tight sudden turns, big climbs, loops, and all kinds of everything in between. Very exciting! I was sitting there nearby watching the cars coming out of the gatehouse and watching them moving out onto the track. They kind of shot out on a level track, then started up a slight incline, then quickly dropped into the ride where all kinds of experiences were to happen. If you've done any dream work you know dreams can be your subconscious speaking to you, communicating important insights and information that can really help you in your life.

So these cars are shooting out of the gatehouse onto the track with these people in them. And I realized, this is just like life. We are shot out into the world where we experience the ups and downs and the twists and turns of life! There are long climbs, amazing views, terrifying drops, deep G-force loaded lows pressing us down into our seats, and we may even get turned upside down. But we are on this ride, like it or not. The cool thing is, once you are on the ride, you get to choose how you will experience it. Now, some people may argue this point, saying there is no way they could ever *enjoy* a rollercoaster ride, or perhaps that they are not at choice for how they experience it. I say fine, you have the experience you are having, but since you are already on this thing, why don't you do whatever you have to do to at least *start* enjoying it. Maybe it's just breathing a bit more. Maybe it's taking in the view. Maybe it's appreciating the incredible *car* you are in and the engineering miracle that it is. I don't know – but there is <u>someplace</u> you can start.

Bottom line is, you're on the ride, it's out of the gatehouse and on the track, and it's going wherever it is going. YOU MIGHT AS WELL ENJOY IT! Advanced NexGen Humans will have their arms in the air laughing as much as possible – recognizing that at some points they get pressed into their seat and will reactively hold on for dear life while their breath gets taken away. That's for real. But it's a ride. And 99.99% of the time, after all the ups and downs, and twists and turns, the car returns to the gatehouse. And in life I would say it's 100% of the time. So what is there to be afraid of? What is there to resist? EVERYONE on the rollercoaster ride will experience the same ups and downs, twists and turns. EVERYONE will experience the same bodily sensations being thrown up and down, left and right, and yes, even moments of disorientation. And EVERYONE has a choice to interpret these *sensations* anyway they want. As a NexGen Human you choose to ALLOW them all, resist nothing, and **GO WITH THE FLOW.**

B<small>REATHE</small>

The emotions intense
I start to resist
I remember to breathe…
and Love flows

G<small>ETTING</small> O<small>UT OF THE</small> R<small>IVER</small>

Now here's where I want to address option number 4: getting out of the river. Note that in our first metaphor of life like a river, it does seem you can get out of the river and stand on the shore. In general I'm certainly a fan of taking in the view and relaxing on the shore. But remember our intention is to "create and have an experience of grace and ease, and one of efficiency; going as far along the river of life as possible with the least amount of effort." Getting out of the river may contribute to some grace and ease, but it clearly does NOT contribute to going as far along the river of life as possible. And in fact, I could argue that it actually reduces your sense of grace and ease, BECAUSE YOU ARE OUT OF THE RIVER OF LIFE! The river of life is just passing you by, and I'm not sure what could be worse than that.

Now in our roller coaster metaphor, "getting out of the river" is a bit more challenging. You'd have to leap from the car, which likely would result in death, or at least significant injury. Not good. In the dream I mentioned, I actually witnessed somebody take out a gun, put it in his mouth and pull the trigger. Committing suicide on the rollercoaster of life. I couldn't believe it. I was shocked. And it made no sense to me. From where I stood, I could see he was going to go around the track, through the ups and downs, the twists and turns, and return safely to the gatehouse. Why would he commit suicide? I know why…because I have been there myself. I know what it's like when life feels so terrible, when the future is so bleak, when each day feels like drudgery, when you're clear that if life is going to be like this each day, you'd rather be dead. It's that simple. LIVING life sucks so much, that being dead, or just *getting out* of the sh*tty experience, is a far more attractive option. I've been there. I *wanted* to be dead, but that's as far as it went.

Somehow, somewhere, deep inside me, I knew it was a rollercoaster ride, and that I was just down on one of those deep G-force loaded lows pressing me into my seat making it difficult for me to breathe.

I hated the experience. I resisted the experience. It "wasn't supposed to be this way." Something was wrong with me. Something was wrong with life! But somehow, somewhere, deep inside me, I knew it was just a rollercoaster ride. A ride that has IT'S OWN momentum. That goes up, and goes down. And that if I could just stay in the car, and keep breathing, I would come through this, and life could be exciting again. And I was right.

No matter how bad our lives might be, we all have experiences of joy and happiness to reflect on. And because of that, we KNOW that life has that to offer us. We KNOW it's there for us because it's been there for us before. We may not know in this moment where or how, but we know it's possible. As a NexGen Human you know to STAY IN THE CAR, and trust the natural momentum of life to move you along. And as it does, practice opening your eyes, putting your hands up in the air, laughing and smiling, screaming on the drops, breathing through the lows, and going for the ride of your life (literally). All the while knowing that a safe return to the gatehouse is a guarantee.

Please note that I am not condemning suicide. I am not here to judge or justify particular choices. Suicide happens. If somehow it happens in your life (to someone else), practice the skills from Chapter 3: embrace and acknowledge life exactly as it IS. Then, choose from there. If everything happens for a reason, and everything is working out perfectly, then if someone commits suicide, it's a denial of reality to say, "That shouldn't have happened." That's a negative judgment of what is – that it was bad and wrong and shouldn't be. The fact is, it DID happen. If this happens in your life, you may become inspired to help others BEFORE they get to that point. Great! You do not have to condemn and negatively judge the past to be inspired to create something new and different (reference NexGen Human skills developed in Chapter 2: Transcend and Include). In fact, the past was absolutely perfect BECAUSE it has inspired you to new action. If those things hadn't happened, you wouldn't be inspired to do what you are doing.

Allowing the Fear

The truth of being human is rarely ever told.

We all experience it, of course, but rarely do we speak it. It's not the kind of thing you find out when you ask, as we all do, "Hey, how are you?" We are expecting a "Great" or a "Fine" <u>regardless</u> of the truth, because frankly, we don't have the time and we don't really want to hear it. And because we ourselves don't want to hear it from others, we ourselves also respond to the question, "Hey, how are you?" with the expected "Great" or "Fine" because we know others don't want to hear it and don't have the time. On top of this is a prevailing illusion that "winners" do not have problems. That winners are always positive, always successful, and never challenged in their lives. We must be strong, like winners. And because we want to be perceived as winners we wear our social masks, hiding the "ugly side" of our life experience, just like everyone else.

I'm not saying wearing social masks is wrong, it certainly facilitates a certain kind of social functioning, but the side effect of pushing the reality of our human experience into the shadows or private world, is that we lose the context for what actually *is* real. And when we lose this context of reality, and look around at the "happy social masks" everyone is wearing, it occurs to us that WE are the outcasts, the broken ones, the unhappy ones.

161

> *In reality, EVERYONE experiences challenges in their life,*
> *EVERYONE has weaknesses, EVERYONE has deep seated fears and*
> *insecurities, and EVERYONE in some way, shape, or form, feels alone*
> *or like an outsider somewhere in their life.*

THIS is life, THIS is the reality of the human experience, *but you have to dig deep to see it for yourself.*

Now, because sharing and discussing our problems, fears, personal challenges, and true feelings is discouraged in society, and because we're all pretending they don't exist, it's a rare teacher that trains us how to BE WITH and ALLOW the "downs" in life. There is very little tolerance for these downs in life. Which, by the way does not make them go away, it just forces them out in other ways. Typical solutions offered are "Don't have them" or "Get out of them asap." The first is unrealistic (Yes or no? Just look in your own life. Have you experienced any downs? I bet the answer is yes. And I'll bet that you'll continue to experience more as you go along in this life. So let's stop pretending). And the second is simply violence – imposing your will on another (yourself) using force – this just pits you against you, and as we know, what we resist, persists.

There is a third way, completely aligned with this chapter *Going with the Flow.* That third way is ALLOWING, or BEING WITH. No one ever says you *can* have the downs, *allow* the downs, and succeed. <u>Everyone is afraid of the downs and is trying to avoid them.</u> To the contrary, I will propose it is in fact, THE path. I think we are grown up enough to hear this - mature enough to hear this now - rather than wanting some fairy tale and avoiding it as if avoiding it will make it not true. This is like pretending gravity doesn't exist and jumping off a building expecting you will fly because you don't believe in gravity. It's fun to fantasize about, but when it comes to actually jumping off the building, I'd suggest you embrace a pretty well tested and validated reality.

Breakdowns are the access to breakthroughs.

- LANDMARK EDUCATION CORPORATION

If you are up to creating anything in your life that is truly challenging, for example your true life's purpose and mission, you will face ups AND downs. And the bigger the game of life you are up to playing, the bigger the ups and downs you will likely experience. It's all part of the Hero's Journey and it's about time we embrace it.

Your ability to ALLOW and BE WITH yourself in the midst of the downs just may be THE most important and powerful skill you develop as a NexGen Human.

In a paradoxical kind of way, this is being weak in a powerful way. We are afraid of being weak. We are afraid of being "out of control." The fact we are afraid is a RED FLAG indicating an opportunity for transformation. The extent to which you can ALLOW and BE WITH this fear in the down times of your life, is the extent to which you will be powerful, and will powerfully <u>move through</u>, these times in your life.

The key to success in both sports and business, and any endeavor in life, is one's ability to bounce back from mistakes.

- DR. BRIAN ALMAN

I once had the feeling my life was like a big jet liner slowly losing altitude on a crash course with the mountains. Here I am on this jet that's "going down" and I'm doing all I can to relax, to feel good, to go with the flow, to release, etc., etc. I was doing everything I knew to transform my experience, but nothing, it seemed, was working. The jet was on a crash course and there was nothing I could do about it, it just kept dropping.

It's a terrifying feeling, and perhaps even made worse since I'm supposed to be an inspiring teacher with my life "all together." However, as this jet was dropping, I realized I am not the teacher that says these moments and experiences in life don't happen. I'm not the teacher that denies life can be difficult and pretends that challenging moments and times don't exist. What I do teach is allowing and trusting, being there and being present. Being strong in your weakest moments *by being weak*, by being scared, by not knowing, and by just allowing. I realized all my <u>striving</u> to escape the terrifying experience and feelings of impending doom was just more of the old fear-based need for control. I was afraid and I didn't like it, so I tried to escape by gaining control. However, this was a form of violence on my self, resisting the natural state I was in, resisting exactly how I was, and trying to force myself to change and feel better.

> *The bottom line is that it's not about <u>not</u> having moments, or times, of weakness and fear. <u>It's about them not having YOU.</u>*

It's still scary, it's still challenging, you will still want to escape it and change it, but there is a part of you that lives on a higher plane of awareness (especially after having read this!), that knows "this too shall pass," the river of life is always flowing, the scenery constantly changing, whether you're paddling or not! It's a practice that gets easier each time as you become aware of those moments of challenge, of fear, when life gets scary, and you can recognize them and *allow them*. As a NexGen Human you can have these experiences without them having you.

THE POWER OF SILENCE

This may seem a little strange to you, but Spirit told me to put in at least one minute of continuous silence into this book. I thought that was a great idea. While Spirit can be found everywhere, there tends to be some places it is more easily found, and silence is definitely one of those places.

Our lives are so full of stuff – not just material physical stuff, but sound and noise as well. How often during our days do we get to really experience a powerful silence?

In this chapter I quote Parker J. Palmer who wrote the book *Let Your Life Speak*. In that book he mentions that the average group of people can tolerate no more than 15 seconds of silence. 15 seconds! Before someone feels compelled to "make some noise" and say something. He points out the belief that if we aren't making noise then NOTHING is happening and likely something is even dying. So we get busy and fill the void with noise.

There's some kind of discomfort that arises in silence, especially in groups – I'm sure you've experienced it, I know I have – we even have a name for it "the uncomfortable silence" as in "an uncomfortable silence fell over the room." But we also have another term "the pregnant pause" that is pointing more toward what I'm talking about here: there is something in the silence that is wanting to be born.

Close your eyes, take a slow deep breath, and give yourself the gift of 60 seconds of silence and just notice what you notice.

As a NexGen Human you want to become very comfortable in the silence - silence of all kinds. And as you calm your mind and become quiet and still yourself, you'll notice a subtle, but VERY POWERFUL presence operating in the silence. I would venture to say it's actually our discomfort and inability to be with this **power** that is present in silence that causes us to flinch. So practice BEING in the silence and being with the POWER of silence. See how fun and powerful it can be.

And guess what? Somehow the jet *magically* got fixed, right in mid air, and I took my seat in first class, knowing with confidence once again, all is well and I'm right on course.

Trust is the Core

A key piece of what we're talking about here is trust, which is at the CORE of going with the flow. Parker J. Palmer wrote a fabulous little book called *Let Your Life Speak*. At one point in this book he outlines what he calls the shadows of leadership. There are five major ones, and I've seen and experienced each of them in myself as well as others. But there was one that particularly struck me; this one was called "Functional Atheism." Palmer described this as a BELIEF that ultimate responsibility for everything rests with us. As he says, "This is the unconscious, unexamined conviction that if anything decent is going to happen here, we are the ones who must make it happen. This belief leads us to impose our will on others, stressing our relationships, sometimes to the point of breaking. It often eventuates in burnout, depression, and despair, as we learn that the world will not bend to our will and we become embittered about that fact. It drives collective frenzy as well and explains why the average group can tolerate no more than fifteen seconds of silence: if we are not making noise, we believe, nothing good is happening and something must be dying." Notice the violence, as previously defined, present in this belief.

The NEED for control lies in distrust, a distrust ultimately in the Universe itself. Where did this distrust come from? Do we distrust the Universe will not beat our hearts for us? Do we distrust the Universe will not provide us air to breathe? Do we have to make the sun rise each day? Do we have to create gravity each day so we don't fly off the planet into space? Do we have to make the rain fall so we don't die of thirst? ALL of life is ultimately a partnership with life itself. Even making money, making products, delivering services, any project or activity you can think of, is actually a partnership with life. As a NexGen Human, as a NexGen *Leader*, you are aware of this fact, and you maximize this partnership for the greatest creation possible.

NexGen Humans know how to go with the flow,
and maximize ALL forces at work through a creative endeavor.

So why don't we trust the Universe? Why are we so often forcing the outcomes, driving to deadlines, producing results, delivering the goods, moving and shaking, making things happen? Why? Fundamentally, this effort filled, forceful, tiring, stressful, struggle, is based in ignorance. It's a lack of awareness of life energy itself. And it's based in fear (that the results will not happen), attachment (that if the results don't happen then bad things WILL happen), and separation (I'm the only one, or we're the only ones who must make this happen – just little ole' me who must shoulder this burden). Fear, attachment, and separation…hmmm. The truth is you DO have a role – it's just that it's not ALL about you. What I'm talking about is awareness and partnership. Maximizing and optimizing your role and the role of the Universe. It's a dance, a dance in awareness that you are part of something far larger than your self (small "s"). And because you are smart, you partner with that something else, you **TRUST** it and work with it to maximize your experience of being alive – and, ultimately, the results you have been <u>inspired</u> to create.

PERMISSION

I give myself permission
Permission to dance wildly through the night
Permission to be bowled over by God's beauty and light
Permission to not know and to learn as I go

To open up and let it flow
However it looks & however it feels
I give myself permission.
In the name of Love…
I give myself permission

The "Need" to Achieve

Now here's another major stumbling block and barrier to *going with the flow*: the need to achieve. Emphasis here is on NEED, as in MUST, as in ATTACHED, as in NO CHOICE. What if you never achieved another thing for the rest of your life? Would that be OK with you? And if you've lived many years in life, and have lots of achievements "behind you," would it be OK if you never achieved any of those things? If you answered no to either or both of these questions (and its likely you did) why is that? Why do we *need* to achieve, and why do we cling to our achievements? (Note that I am including winning in this definition of achievement). What might it be like to be free of this need and attachment to achievement and winning? Contemplate that for a moment.

Where does this need, this drive, this attachment, come from? I invite you to take a look. I bet if you look closely, once again, it has its roots in fear. Fear of not being accepted, fear of dying (the need to survive), fear of being unworthy, fear of being unhappy, fear of not being enough, fear of rejection, fear of not making a difference, fear of having end of life regrets, fear of not knowing who you are, fear, fear, and more fear.

To the extent you are not OK with not achieving or winning, you have
one of these fears underlying and driving your life experience.

"You" are not free.

What if you just let go of this need, this drive, this attachment, this fear, what would happen? Would you lose your identity and become a "tub-of-goo," a lazy, good-for-nothing derelict, a tax on society? What if living a successful life has nothing to do with *achievement?* What if what you are supposed to be doing in life is happening no matter what you do or achieve? That success in life is already guaranteed REGARDLESS of your achievements?

Listen to your mind right now and what it might be saying in response to these statements – is it accepting them with curiosity and openness, or is it more along the lines of "This is a bunch of crap, achievement and winning is key, I *have to* win and I *have to* achieve." Notice if you feel resistance in some other form. Perhaps your mind is like mine and wants to know where inspiration would come from if not from the root of "fear of not achieving?" Or perhaps it wonders what you would do and who you would be? Or what others would think of you? Or what you would think of you?

> *I invite you to let go of your need and your drive to achieve*
> *– even just for a moment –*
> *and explore what life might be like if you didn't "have to."*

What might arise (naturally, of course) from that level of freedom? What might be available that is not currently available? I caution you to not *expect* something to arise (for in that expectation is again that root of fear), but rather look with the eyes of a true explorer – one that is coming to a mountaintop for the first time and has no idea what he/she will see on the other side. Look with those eyes, and I guarantee you will see what there is to see. Can you sense it now?

Inspired – motivated by divine influence.

QUESTIONS FOR REFLECTION

+ Overall in your life, how much are you paddling against the flow, just floating along, or paddling with the flow? Write down a ratio. How might you like to change that? What are some actions you can take to get this more in balance?

+ Where do you distrust the Universe? How might you live if you trusted more?

+ Where do you try to "force nature" to your own demise? (Do you try to "force" the plants in your garden to grow faster than nature allows? That's simply frustrating. Yes, optimize the seed selection, the soil composition, the water, and the sun exposure, THEN LET NATURE DO THE REST IN IT'S OWN TIME).

OPPORTUNITIES FOR ACTION

+ Meditation is an excellent practice for going with the flow. Take up a meditation practice and cultivate the peace, trust, and knowing that can result from quieting your mind and developing a deep and rich inner life experience.

+ Take the HeartMath *Voyage to Heart Intelligence* and learn how to stay connected to your Heart. This will place you in the flow of life, connected, present, and authentically inspired in each moment (see "Powerful Resources" at the end of Chapter VIII *Partnership with Source* for more information).

Powerful Resources

+ Book: "The Type-Z Guide to Success: A Lazy Persons Manifesto for Wealth and Fulfillment" by Marc Allen (see resources in Chapter VII for an expanded description of this book).

+ Book: "Sabbath: Restoring the Sacred Rhythm of Rest" by Wayne Muller – the perspective this book restores is so needed for us at this time in history. Read this book and relax into the beautiful, mystical, and natural, ever-changing cycles and rhythms of life. It will help you see that *doing nothing* is a very powerful practice that will inspire and enliven all parts of your life.

+ Book: "Busting Loose From the Money Game – Mind Blowing Strategies for Changing the Rules of a Game You Can't Win" by Robert Scheinfeld – Robert outlines a bold new vision and model for powerful living. When I first read this book I got very irritated, disoriented, and a bit confused – however I knew that was a good sign I had beliefs ingrained the book was challenging. Sure enough. Get ready for a wild ride and an amazing new perspective on life that is ultimately empowering and freeing.

+ Book: "Transitions: Making Sense of Life's Changes – Strategies for Coping with the Difficult, Painful, and Confusing Times in Your Life" by William Bridges (see resources in Chapter V for an expanded description of this book).

✦ Book: "Let Your Life Speak – Listening for the Voice of Vocation" by Parker J. Palmer – a great little read with lots of wisdom. Highly recommended.

✦ Beyond Belief Audio Program: "Journey to Source & Vision Quest" www.GoBeyondBelief.com/products.php (see website or resources in Chapter VIII for an expanded description of this audio program).

✦ Beyond Belief Audio Program: "Love Expander & Ascension Accelerator" www.GoBeyondBelief.com/products.php (see website or resources in Chapter III for an expanded description of this audio program).

✦ Beyond Belief Audio Program: "Shift It – Accessing the Gift Within" www.GoBeyondBelief.com/products.php (see website or resources in Chapter III for an expanded description of this audio program).

Chapter X

Walking the Path

Walking the path is a day to day experience. It happens, as we saw in Chapter VI, One Step at a Time. On the path there are bad days and great days, and all kinds of days in between. However, I have found that walking with others not only makes it a whole lot more enjoyable, it also makes possible things that just aren't possible when you are walking alone. We are on this planet with other people for a reason! If life was meant to be lived alone, you would BE alone. But alas, at last count, there are some 6 billion of us walking around!

As a NexGen Human engaging your Hero's Journey,
moving from Isolation to Integration,
finding your friends, the folks on your team, is essential.

If you have been resonating with the messages of this book, then you will likely find some kindred souls via the resources listed at the end of this chapter. You've got to step up, step out, and reach out. Otherwise nobody knows who you are, what you stand for, and what you need – and *you* have no idea what you are missing! When *who I was* started becoming

EXPANSION AND CONTRACTION

When "walking the path" of the NexGen Human, as I just mentioned, you'll have good days and bad days, and all kinds of days in between. Being in a community can greatly support your ability to be with the ups and downs of life – because when you are down, someone else might be up, and may be able to provide you the light, compassion, and support you may need in the dark or down times of your life.

One time when I was frustrated and struggling to maximize my output and productivity under the false belief that I should operate like a machine and produce results 24/7, 365 days a year, I was trying to figure out what increased my energy and what decreased my energy. So I created a spreadsheet – on that spreadsheet I listed out about 15 or 20 different factors that I suspected had an impact on my energy level, things like amount of sleep, types and amount of food, water intake, caffeine intake, exercise, work demands, amount of outdoor exposure including sunlight, the experience of stressful or inspiring events in my life, etc., etc. I had it all on there. Then I set up a 6 month timeline and I captured each day what I did and experienced in these areas. I then rated my energy level for the day on a scale of 1 to 5, with 1 being super low, basically dragging my ass through the day, and 5 being outstanding and amazing, effortlessly and magically moving through my day.

You know what I found? No matter what I did, no matter how much demand there was on me, my energy CYCLED. There was a very pronounced weekly cycle, where on a pretty routine 7 day cycle I had 2 days of very high 4 or 5 level energy, 2 days of very low, 1 or 2 level energy, and about 3 days of average or "3" level energy. I was blown away to see this cycle running through my life, REGARDLESS of how much caffeine I had, how good my diet was, how much sleep I was getting, whether I exercised or not, my demands at work, etc. No matter what was going on in my life and what I was doing, my energy levels were cycling in this sinusoidal like fashion from high through the middle, down to low, through the middle, and back to high again.

Ever since then I've noticed this is a feature of life itself. You can see it in the seasons – with winter being the low energy, summer being the high energy, and fall and spring being the transitional, or average energy months. Spring is where the energy is coming up, and fall is where the energy is going back down.

You can see these cycles in the dynamic of a day – nighttime is where the energy is lowest, then there is the dawn where energy is rising, there is midday where energy is the highest, then sunset where the energy is decreasing, on it's way back to the low energy of nighttime. You can see this in your breath cycle. Most people think of the breath as only a two phase process – in and out – but it's actually a 4 phase process when you include the 2 moments of transition between the in and out phases. So when you've fully exhaled, that would be the lowest energy point (equivalent to winter), then the transitional moment when you stop exhaling and begin to inhale would be where the energy turns and begins to go up (equivalent to spring), and then when you have inhaled and your lungs are full that would be the peak energy (or summer), and then the transitional moment when you stop inhaling and begin to exhale that would be where the energy turns and begins back down (or fall).

My point is, energy cycles, in the Universe AND in you. It expands and it contracts. And this is NORMAL. To the extent you are aware of this, you can be fully present in both the expansion AND contraction stages – to partner with it. Note that it's the contraction phase that we tend to resist – it feels like death to us, and we are afraid of death – we don't like to think of or experience things dying, so we try to be busy ALL THE TIME. Doing this we totally miss and disrespect the opportunity that the contraction cycle is. It's from the contraction that expansion can even take place – you cannot have one without the other.

As a NexGen Human you are wise to this expansion and contraction. You recognize it is a normal and natural part of the path and life itself. And because of that, you embrace the contraction, knowing that is what there is to do, and knowing that expansion is sure to follow. The tide goes out, and the tide comes in – it goes out, and it comes in, it goes out, and it comes in. If you pay attention you'll see this pattern in YOUR life too, and you'll be powerful through all phases, resisting nothing and allowing it all.

more clear, I at first felt quite isolated. But then, when I opened up to it and started looking, I found some fabulous organizations, practices, and people, that are now like family.

You know you've found them when you are accepted for who you are, you naturally fit in, and it's natural for you to be yourself, say what you are thinking and feeling, and grow in the relationship.

DEVELOPING CLARITY - STRENGTHENING YOUR YES AND NO

Developing clarity and strengthening your Yes and your No, is a very important skill of a NexGen Human. As your mission becomes clearer and your confidence in *who you are* becomes greater and greater, your ability to identify, attract, and engage *people on your path* gets stronger and stronger. On the flip side, your ability to know who and what is NOT on your path gets stronger and stronger as well. And eventually, what comes along with this knowledge is your ability to say NO to who and what is *not* on your path. The funny thing is, people and opportunities NOT on your path will likely keep showing up, especially in the early stages of engaging your mission. What these become are opportunities for you to continue embracing who and what you are, by saying NO to who and what is not on your path.

Eventually you get to a point in life where it's about living your mission and making your contribution to the world. This is what becomes most important.

If something or someone does not support, or is not aligned with this highest purpose and vision for your life, then it serves no one (including them!) to spend your time and energy with them or it. Having this kind of capacity requires that you are very clear on your own authentic life path and mission. When you have clarity on this, it becomes a lot easier to say YES and NO to best facilitate your service and gifts into the world. Remember Principle #4 from Chapter VII, *your* people on your path (friends, contributors, collaborators, customers, etc.) will NOT show up until <u>YOU</u> do.

The Passion Test is one of the best methods I have ever experienced for gaining clarity on your authentic life path and mission. The Passion Test will help you define and prioritize the things you are most passionate about in life. Defining your most important passions will enable you to make choices that support living from your passions. Chris and Janet Attwood, authors of the book *The Passion Test*, point out that one of the most important keys to living a life of passion is "Whenever you are faced with a decision, a choice, or an opportunity, choose in favor of your passions." First of all, this requires that you know what your passions are, and second it requires that whenever you are faced with a decision, a choice, or an opportunity, you empower yourself to choose in favor of your passions. By consistently choosing in favor of your passions you will soon find you are living a passion filled life (see "Powerful Resources" at the end of Chapter VII for a more full description of this book and process).

EXPANDED CAPACITIES IN THE PRESENCE OF OTHERS

One very interesting element of community is that "who we are with others, is not who we are when alone." Think about it, who you are, the thoughts you are having, the things you say, the things you do, are different depending on who you are in the presence of. This is a very interesting characteristic of relationships. We've all been around people who make us feel good or who inspire us. And on the other hand, we've all been around people who depress us and suck the energy out of us. Clearly, we are affected by the people we are interacting with.

In the Spring 1996 issue of *The Noetic Sciences Review,* Margaret Wheatley (Organizational Consultant and author of *Leadership and the New Science: Learning About Organization from an Orderly Universe*) wrote an article about the hidden intelligence orchestrating and organizing all things in the Universe. And in this article one of the things she pointed out is that *who we are with others* or *who we are in community* is different than who we are when alone.

You cannot understand the power of the individual by assessing or understanding who they are when alone.

You have to look at them when in community and in relationship with others! However, what she pointed out, was that "none of the personality assessors or indicators (e.g. Myers-Briggs) let us know who or what we are capable of being when we are in community with one another."

She provides a great example of 20 foot tall termite towers on the Australian savanna. When entomologists study the individual termite what they find is they are only capable of digging dirt piles. However these 20 foot towers are amazingly complex feats of engineering, built on a north-south axis, with tunnels and arches inside designed to move air into a darkened interior where it is cooler. "The nests are also designed to move moisture in so the termites can farm a form of fungi they require for digestion. These are very sophisticated structures."

Entomologists looked for years for the leader, for the engineer, for the "brains" behind the operation. But they never found one. What they found when they looked closer was an *emergent capacity* in the termites that was only present when in community. If you looked just at an individual termite, all you saw was that they could dig. But when they got together, new capacities for building began to emerge. "Isolated, they barely have any significance. But as a coordinated group they perform like a hive-mind. Like neurons, they emit chemicals for communication...they're very tuned in...and they respond."

While this article by Margaret was mostly about leaderless organizations and the self-organizing principles of the Universe – the main take away for a NexGen Human is to realize that:

Your capacities with others are different (and likely far greater with "your people") than when you are alone.

A Long Term Practice

One of the most powerful communities and practices I have discovered is called *Integral Transformative Practice* or ITP for short. This is a long term practice for transformation developed by human potential pioneers George Leonard and Michael Murphy. Michael Murphy is one of the founders of the Esalen Institute (the west coast center for the human potential movement for more than 40 years located in beautiful Big Sur, California), and George Leonard was President of The Esalen Institute for a number of years. Over the years these two saw pretty much everything when it came to programs and processes for human transformation.

On January 4, 1992 they embarked on a research study they called *Integral Transformative Practice* with 36 people that met every Saturday morning for 11 months. In 1993 a second group met for 10 consecutive months. They decided they would forgo the spectacular "gee-whiz" experiences they knew they could facilitate, feeling they only gave the *illusion* of significant change and could even interfere with lasting, long-term transformation. Rather, they held a strong belief in the "transformative power and sacredness of life's quiet virtues, including intellectual curiosity and integrity, a sense of the spiritual, unconditional love, healthy exercise, and a devotion to practice," they "were in it for the long run." "The practice would be *integral* in that it would involve and seek to integrate body, mind, heart, and soul. It would be *transformative* in that it would aim toward positive, long-term personal change."

The experiment was successful and demonstrated that statistically significant transformations of mind, body, heart and soul are all possible through this practice. After more than 4 years of practicing ITP myself, I can heartily support its transformative impact.

One of the most important distinctions of the ITP practice is the notion of a <u>long term commitment</u> over time. Inside a long term commitment of practice and **walking the path** the normal ups and downs that every human being experiences can be held. The long term aspect provides the container and context in which these ups and downs are defined. They no longer sit separately by themselves, blowing you off course when they hit, because they are just *part of the path*. You may experience apathy for a day, a week, or even a month, but inside the context of a long term practice and path, you can still be strong and better weather the storm. Your journey, your commitment, AND WHO YOU ARE, is far greater than any momentary storm.

ESTABLISHING A PRACTICE

I cannot overemphasize how important having a long term practice is. It's inside of this long term context that your true transformation and evolution will be most powerfully facilitated. In a long term practice you have the time to experience what does and doesn't work for you, what is and is not efficient for you, and then tune and optimize.

As we've discovered throughout this book, transformation happens over time. You want to be on a path of regular practice that marks your way, that guides and supports you, that keeps you and your evolution on track. It's like creating a groove in a piece of wood with a rock, or perhaps on a piece of glass with a diamond – the first time you practice you just scratch the surface of the wood or glass – but then each time you practice, over and over again, you deepen that groove, and those things you are working on. Your connection to Source and Heart Wisdom, seeing the good in everything, going with the flow, transcending your subconscious limiting beliefs, embracing the contraction and low energy times in your life, and expressing and creating your authentic life purpose, all eventually become the

natural path for divine energy flow in your life.

For your practice to have deep transformational value it must happen independent of what is going on in your life. If life rules you, you will soon stop your practice. However, if you engage your practice <u>independent</u> of the conditions in your life, or even <u>along with</u> the circumstances and conditions of your life, you can persist. This means you choose to do your practice for no reason and you do it no matter what.

Actually you can look at your life as your ultimate long term practice. Over your years on this earth you discover what works and doesn't work for you, making adjustments, learning and deepening your connection to Source, until you ultimately and literally **do** dissolve into the oneness. Your long term practice can be a microcosm of this ultimate and *real* long term practice of your life – becoming more free, present, powerful, and joy-filled – while still alive and animating your physical form.

And don't be afraid to try out different practices and to do what works for you. I've engaged many different forms and my transformational practice has evolved as I embrace what works for me and let go of what doesn't. Know

> that some things may work for you and be very powerful at one stage of your life, but then you grow beyond it and are ready for something else. Don't feel like you have to select something and stay with it forever. Be free to evolve and engage and create what works for you.
>
> The most important thing is to create and engage a long term transformational practice.

I have a 20 year calendar on the wall in my office. This is a very powerful visual aid that provides a long term context. Even if you are 80 or 90 years old you can still have a 20 year calendar. You are never too old to have a 20 year calendar and put your life in the long term context it deserves to be in. In this longer context, the "fear-based-urgency" tends to lose its power, and you realize just how much time there really is. With authentic, diligent, conscious practice there is plenty of time for the unfolding of your life. SO MUCH can happen over 1 or 2 years that when you see them in the context of 20 years, my God, you can literally do ANYTHING. Borrowing again from Marc Allen, affirm: MY LIFE IS PERFECTLY UNFOLDING, IN A RELAXED AND EASY WAY, IN ITS OWN PERFECT TIME FOR THE HIGHEST GOOD OF ALL. Because it is!

The Forever Path of Evolution

Every day is a new day. The world is constantly changing. What was not possible yesterday could very well be possible today – both for yourself and in general for the world. Most people learn something once and assume it's true for the rest of their lives. Don't get stuck in the past. Always be willing to update what you know to be "true," because each day truly brings new possibilities. Just because someone has "a lot of experience" does not mean they are right – one way to look at "a lot of experience" is knowledge of HOW THINGS WORKED AT ONE TIME IN THEIR EXPERIENCE, which they continue to prove over and over to themselves, and anyone else who will listen, time and time again.

"Experience" can become baggage from the past that severely limits what is possible today.

Consider that what may be true at one time and one level of consciousness may no longer be true at another. As Edgar Mitchell, Apollo 14 astronaut and founder of the Institute of Noetic Sciences has said: "Today's truths are likely tomorrow's myths." And as Willis Harmon, past President of the Institute of Noetic Sciences and author of *Global Mind Change* has often been quoted as saying: "Perhaps the only limits to the mind are those we *believe* in."

What this means is that to evolve and move forward, you must let go of those things that previously may have served you, things that may have been your greatest strengths or touchstones of reality, your strongest *beliefs*. Initially these will be your self-limiting beliefs from childhood, but as you grow and adopt new beliefs, eventually even those will become old beliefs that hold you back from new levels of awareness. In my experience, transformation is typically preceded by discomfort, frustration, and even anger. This is mostly due to old belief systems being challenged. As scary as it may seem, as we have seen throughout this book, what there is to "do" is <u>embrace</u> your fears, transcend and include them. As you practice the skills of a NexGen Human, this process of evolution itself will get easier and easier. Eventually you'll be able to easily adopt new beliefs and let go of those no longer serving you. Talk about freedom!

THE HERO'S JOURNEY

As we wind up this chapter, *Walking the Path*, I'd like to further distinguish the Modern Age Hero's Journey – the Journey of a NexGen Human.

One way to look at the Hero's Journey is through four different stages – in some aspects this is similar to the Four Stage Learning Model we looked at in Chapter VI, but in most aspects its quite distinct – so keep these two models separate in your consciousness.

The first stage of the Hero's Journey can be seen as Unconscious Connection. In this state you are connected to all the things in your life and you don't even realize there is any other way to be, it just IS the way it is, and in that sense you are unconscious of it. Then at some point in this stage, an impulse arises that causes you to initiate separation – this is not a deliberate conscious decision, just for some reason, whatever reason, an impulse arises that initiates your separation. This stage I call Unconscious Separation. You initiate separation from whatever you have been connected with, but it's done on an unconscious level.

As you move into this separation, what arises next is an awareness of "how things used to be"…now that you are no longer connected with that which you have separated from, you become aware of, or conscious of, your separation. This is stage three, Conscious Separation. It is in this stage you distinguish your Self, you distinguish who you are as *distinct from* that which you have separated from. After experiencing this stage for some time, a yearning for connection then arises and you begin your journey home. Having defined yourself anew, you then consciously connect, or re-connect, with that you had separated from, initiating a whole new appreciation and experience of that which you are now newly, and now consciously, connected to.

So the four stages in this model of the Hero's Journey are: Unconscious Connection, Unconscious Separation, Conscious Separation, and finally Conscious Connection.

We can see this model operating in many facets of life. First, can you see it operating in our lives as children becoming adults? When we are born we are Unconsciously Connected to our parents, just happily going about our lives, not KNOWING anything different. Then at some point, an impulse arises which unconsciously initiates the beginning of our separation, where we start to define ourselves as separate beings from our parents. Then at some point we begin consciously choosing our separation, probably starting right around teenager years, really wanting to be free and independent. And this goes on for some time as we distinguish who we are as separate from our parents. And then, at some point (some later than others, and for some never at all) we begin consciously choosing to connect again with our parents – bringing the power of our own independence and identity into the relationship – and experience a new level of appreciation with and for our parents.

These same four stages can be seen in our spiritual growth and evolution – which is really what this book, and a NexGen Human, is all about. We are born in pure Unconscious Connection and oneness with Great Spirit. Then our ego begins its development and we unconsciously begin our separation, developing and using words like "I" "me" "it" "them". Then we fully embrace this separation, consciously creating our identities and really distinguishing who we are as separate from Source. Then at some point this becomes painful as our separation becomes no longer empowering, but rather limiting, and we sense that something is missing from our lives. It's <u>that</u> yearning that initiates Stage 4, Conscious Connection. As we return to our connection with Spirit, having experienced being away and having worked hard at creating ourselves

as uniquely separate, we now experience our connection with Great Spirit in which we are newly and consciously, as if for the first time, connected to.

This is the Hero's Journey in the context of Spiritual transformation and evolution.

So where are you in this model? My guess is that you are likely somewhere between stages 3 and 4. This book is mostly designed to help people waking up in Stage 3 – people becoming conscious of their separation, and noticing that something is missing from their lives, but they aren't quite sure what it is. If that's you, then you've come to the right place, and I've got good news for you – you don't have to start your Hero's Journey. Why? Because you're already on it, and you always have been – it's just that you've been unconsciously on your Journey. Notice that the first two stages happen unconsciously.

Perhaps this book marks the beginning of the CONSCIOUS stages of your Journey – stages 3 and 4, and the beginning of your journey back home.

This is the evolutionary opportunity of our time, of your time, as a NexGen Human.

The Fire of Transformation

One of my favorite experiences is sitting next to and looking into a real fire. There is something magical and mesmerizing about fire. If you think about it, it's one place where you can easily see and witness the process of transformation – the transformation of wood into ashes, and the release of its energy into the beautiful, ever changing, form of flame. While this is *always* happening in *all* things in life, there are not very many places where you can see it so clearly. As a NexGen Human on the path of our Hero's Journey, this is what we are doing too: transforming, releasing our flames, warming the world and burning brightly for all to see, and eventually ending, blissfully in ashes.

Warming Myself by the Fire

To warm myself by the fire
Is to enrich my soul
Is to spend a few minutes with an old friend
To catch the blink of an eye
To witness divine release
To feel the knowing presence of the one
To be
The knowing presence of the one
Dancing light all knowing
Dancing light all becoming
I love it
I feel it
I am it
Warming myself by the fire

Questions for Reflection

+ Who are your people? Where do you think you might find them?
+ What do you think are some of the key practices for you to include on your own long-term path of personal growth and evolution?

Perhaps consider some of the following:
+ Professional coaching
+ Regular meditation
+ Yoga
+ Martial Arts
+ Journaling
+ Participating in ITP or another supportive community
+ Seminars and workshops (ongoing learning)
+ Inspiring books and tapes
+ HeartMath practice
+ Regular exercise or physical movement of some kind
+ An energizing diet with lots of water and live foods
+ Regular fun and play

Opportunities for Action

+ Who and what in your life right now does not support your highest vision of yourself? List out these people, activities, and things. Decide right now to give less of your time, attention, and energy to these things on your path that are not serving you (nor is it serving them!).
+ Who and what in your life right now does support your highest vision of yourself? List out these people, activities, and things. Decide right now to give more of your time, attention, and energy

to these things on your path that are serving and supporting the highest vision of yourself.

Powerful Resources

* Book: "The Life We Are Given – A Long Term Program for Realizing the Potential of Body, Mind, Heart, and Soul" by George Leonard and Michael Murphy

* Integral Transformative Practice International - www.ITP-Life. org

* Institute of Noetic Sciences – www.Noetic.org

* United Centers for Spiritual Living (previously known as Church of Religious Science) – home of Science of Mind – www. ReligiousScience.org

* Association for Global New Thought – www.AGNT.org

* Beyond Belief Audio Program: Deep Relaxation & Power Visioning Process www.GoBeyondBelief.com/products.php

Chapter XI

THE NEXGEN HUMAN –
SUMMARY OF TRAITS

So here we are, at the end of the beginning. If you've read all of this book, you've been on quite a journey:

- We started by stepping onto the path of the Modern Age Hero's Journey, going from poor suffering bastard to divinely inspired being, and distinguished *The Critical Skill* for the 21ˢᵗ Century; the ability to consciously and consistently connect with the intelligent power of the Universe.

- This was followed by taking stock of our current situation and learning to celebrate and integrate our past, learning to *Transcend and Include* it as we expand into new visions for our lives.

- This led us to *A Good Place to Start* where we began to see the natural tendency of our mind to focus on fear and learned to appreciate the benefits of proactively cultivating our focus on the good in our lives.

- From here we distinguished *The Great Transformation* as an essential step of taking back the power in our lives and no longer playing the victim to anyone or anything.

- Next, we saw that *It's All About Evolution*; evolving ourselves to higher and wider planes of consciousness in our lives, working through our own subconscious limiting beliefs, embracing our fears, expanding our ability to love ourselves and others, and becoming the clear channel for life force energy we are destined to be.

- Then we looked at how life unfolds *One Step at a Time* and learned to have patience with ourselves, to stop "shouting at the sequoia" and to trust and allow our growth and expansion to occur naturally.

- Next we came to appreciate *Your Place in the Universe and The Power of Your Purpose* and saw that each and every one of us has a reason for being here that is at the same time our greatest opportunity for personal evolution and the key to our highest levels of fulfillment and satisfaction.

- Then we dove deeper into the critical skill of establishing a strong *Partnership with Source* and learned that through the <u>heart</u> - God, Universal Intelligence, Great Spirit, Source - speaks to us most clearly.

- From there, with a strong connection to Source established, we saw that our ability to *Go with the Flow* is increased as we learn to trust Universal Energy and relax into the river of life, powerfully being with and allowing both the good times <u>and</u> the tough times.

- And finally, in *Walking the Path*, we discovered the importance of a long term commitment to practice and the power of connecting in community.

- And that then brings us to here, to this summary chapter, tying it all together into what we now know is a *NexGen Human*. You ARE a NexGen Human.

In closing, I would like to end where we began, with the following prayer that came to me one night in a dream. It is my wish for you that this *Prayer for a NexGen Human* fully manifest in your life:

Prayer for a NexGen Human

I embrace the adventure that is my life
I rejoice in its challenges
I rejoice in its opportunities
Through all my ups and through all my downs
I am strengthened on my journey
As I deepen my Connections
I unfold and discover
Who I am
And deliver my gifts
To the world
I embrace the adventure that is my life!

Epilogue

GOING BEYOND BELIEF

Realizing it is our own *beliefs* that are limiting our growth, happiness, and evolution as a species, several years ago I formed a California-based company called Beyond Belief to support people in *Going Beyond Belief*. The essence of a NexGen Human is core to the Purpose and Vision of Beyond Belief:

BEYOND BELIEF PURPOSE

The purpose of Beyond Belief is to maximize your co-creative partnership with Source and the metaphysical forces of the Universe to uniquely and joyfully live your life's purpose.

BEYOND BELIEF VISION

There is a higher power and intelligence guiding the unfolding of the Universe. As human beings we play an important and integral role in this divine unfolding, perhaps now more than ever. As part of this unfolding, we as human beings have been given the unique gift and power of choice - we can choose our level of participation and partnership with the higher power in the unfolding of the Universe. At Beyond Belief, we have chosen to maximize our partnership with divine intelligence and be a vehicle through which others can choose and maximize their own partnership with higher power and the many metaphysical forces available to them in the Universe.

Through its various programs, products, and materials, Beyond Belief integrates the emotional and spiritual intelligence of religions, philosophies, and cultures developed over thousands of years, with the intellectual power and understanding of emerging new sciences, especially Quantum Physics, and other new paradigms, processes, and discoveries. This is done on an individual-by-individual basis, using all six senses, to literally and powerfully integrate these two worlds, metaphysical and physical, in the personal reality of each human being we work with.

This is done to enable and maximize what we believe is the primary purpose of life, to evolve, and through that evolution, to manifest our personal destinies. Everyone has a purpose they are here to create and manifest. We have bodies, minds, hearts, and souls to enable us to create and experience our unique divine purpose on this physical plane. To not manifest one's personal destiny is to suffer. Beyond Belief relieves suffering by empowering people in their own personal expression and manifestation and optimizes their role as a unique doorway between the metaphysical and physical realities.

Beyond Belief is a growing international community of practitioners in the world of Personal Evolution and Self Actualization. These are people committed to maximizing their contribution to the evolution of the planet by maximizing their own evolutionary development. By delivering the best of both time-tested and emerging new paradigms, Beyond Belief keeps its members on their cutting edge of evolution.

Ultimately, Beyond Belief is a co-creative partner for evolutionary human beings. Human beings living at choice in the world, aware that they are responsible for and are creating their experience in the world. These are people going beyond fixing symptoms who are now going to the Source of experience. Through it's community of members and through it's own innovative training programs, products, and materials Beyond Belief has ignited a revolution of personal freedom and response-ability. Members of the Beyond Belief community represent a critical mass of people who are actively engaged in the realization that everything anyone needs and wants to experience lies within.

Final Note

Everything has its place in the Universe and serves a purpose. Life is a journey, and for every step you take, there is always another waiting to be taken - no matter how big your game becomes, there is always a bigger one to play - and each book, training program, and expert has a unique place along the pathway for those that seek to learn and grow. It is my intention that Beyond Belief take its unique place in the lives it is meant to serve and I am committed that those lives are uplifted and expanded, ready for the next step and the bigger game.

Please contact me if I may be of service to you in the fulfillment of your life. It would be my pleasure and honor.

Thank you for being your amazing self!

NAMASTE & BLESSINGS,

ROGER KENNETH MARSH
PLEASANTON, CALIFORNIA
JUNE, 2008

Path of the NexGen Human

As a reward for purchasing and reading this book, please visit this special page on my website, accessible only to readers of this book, to receive very special pricing on my breakthrough program Path of the NexGen Human:

www.GoBeyondBelief.com/specialoffer.php

As great as books are, they can only take you so far down the road of personal growth and development. Leading institutions have realized that real transformation requires focused effort supported OVER TIME. It's a process of engaging and strengthening habits, practices, and ways of being and thinking that are supportive to you and your life. The Path of the NexGen Human provides the tools, the support, and the structure you need to make the changes you want. Conveniently facilitated via phone and the Internet, this 6 month program includes:

+ The Passion Test
+ The HeartMath Voyage to Heart Intelligence
+ Five Beyond Belief transformational audio programs (Journey to Source, Power Visioning, Love Expander, Shift-It!, and Affirmation Activation)
+ The 90 day "NexGen Human Guide for Daily Practice"
+ A community of like-minded people via membership in the NexGen Human Online Network
+ Monthly NexGen Human teleconference calls and Podcasts

Through this program you will put the wisdom of this book into practice in your life. You will develop habits, new skills, and ways of seeing and being in the world that support you in living a life that you love. This is where "the rubber meets the road" and good intentions become reality. You will find your passions, connect to your heart, and experience fulfillment in whole new ways! Your new world is waiting! Visit www. GoBeyondBelief.com/specialoffer.php

4128753

Made in the USA
Lexington, KY
23 December 2009